DK BACKPACK BOOKS

1,001 FACTS ABOUT
DINOSAURS

SAUROPELTA

IGUANODON

MEGALOSAURUS TOOTH

BACKPACK BOOKS

1,001 FACTS ABOUT

DINOSAURS

Written by
NEIL CLARK
and WILLIAM LINDSAY
With additional material
from Dougal Dixon

HYPSILOPHODON

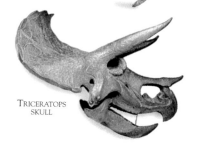

TRICERATOPS
SKULL

STEGOSAURUS

DK PUBLISHING, INC.

LONDON, NEW YORK, MUNICH,
MELBOURNE AND DELHI

Editor Simon Mugford
Designer Dan Green
Senior editor Andrew Macintyre
Design manager Jane Thomas
Production Nicola Torode
With thanks to the original team
Editor Bernadette Crowley
Art editors Ann Cannings
Sheilagh Noble
Senior editor Susan McKeever
Senior art editor Helen Senior
Picture research Caroline Brooke

First American Edition, 2002

2468109753

Published in the United States by
DK Publishing, Inc.,
375 Hudson Street,
New York, NY 10014

A catalog record for this book is available from
the Library of Congress

ISBN 0-7894-8448-X

Color reproduction by Colourscan
Printed and bound in Singapore

See our complete product line at
www.dk.com

CONTENTS

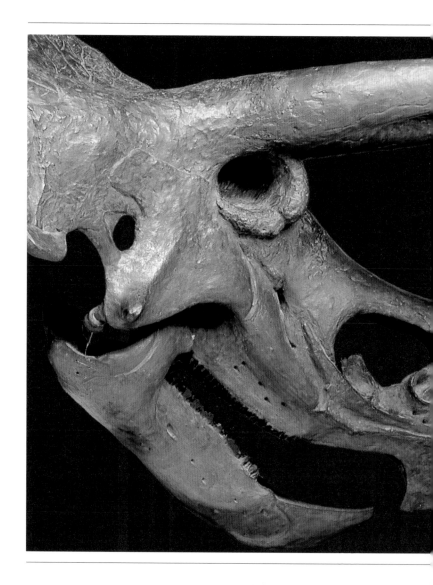

INTRODUCTION TO DINOSAURS

WHAT ARE DINOSAURS?

ABOUT 225 MILLION YEARS AGO, a new group of reptiles appeared on Earth. Like all reptiles, they had waterproof, scaly skin and young that hatched from eggs. These were the dinosaurs. For the next 160 million years they ruled the Earth, before finally becoming extinct.

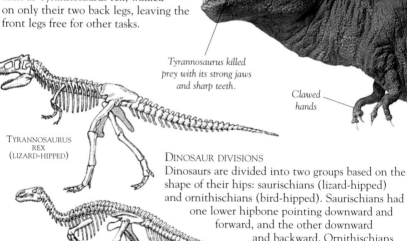

Powerful neck muscles were needed for ripping flesh from prey.

LAND LEGS
Dinosaurs were land animals – they could not swim or fly. All dinosaurs had four limbs, but many, such as Tyrannosaurus rex, walked on only their two back legs, leaving the front legs free for other tasks.

Tyrannosaurus killed prey with its strong jaws and sharp teeth.

Clawed hands

TYRANNOSAURUS
REX
(LIZARD-HIPPED)

DINOSAUR DIVISIONS
Dinosaurs are divided into two groups based on the shape of their hips: saurischians (lizard-hipped) and ornithischians (bird-hipped). Saurischians had one lower hipbone pointing downward and forward, and the other downward and backward. Ornithischians had their two lower hipbones pointing downward and backward.

IGUANODON
(BIRD-HIPPED)

Period	Millions of years ago	Examples of dinosaurs from each period	
CRETACEOUS	65-145		Triceratops
JURASSIC	145-208		Stegosaurus
TRIASSIC	208-245		Herrerasaurus

TIME LINES

Dinosaurs lived through three periods in the Earth's history – Triassic, Jurassic, and Cretaceous. Different species of dinosaur lived and died throughout these three periods. Each species may have survived for only 2-3 million years.

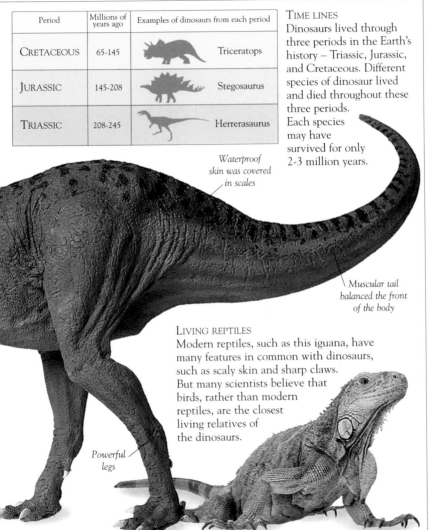

Waterproof skin was covered in scales

Muscular tail balanced the front of the body

LIVING REPTILES

Modern reptiles, such as this iguana, have many features in common with dinosaurs, such as scaly skin and sharp claws. But many scientists believe that birds, rather than modern reptiles, are the closest living relatives of the dinosaurs.

Powerful legs

Types of dinosaur

Dinosaur designs were varied and spectacular. A group of dinosaurs called the sauropods were the largest land animals that ever lived. The smallest dinosaurs were dog-sized. Large or small, all would have been wary of hungry meat eaters. Some dinosaurs had armored skin for protection. Others were fast runners and could escape predators by fleeing to safer ground.

DINOSAUR TERROR
Tyrannosaurus rex and other fierce meat eaters had huge, sharp teeth with which they killed prey.

HERBIVORES
There were many more herbivores (plant eaters) than carnivores (meat eaters) in the dinosaur world. A herbivore called Stegosaurus had a sharp beak for cropping leaves off plants.

ONE OF THE BIGGEST
Heavier than eight elephants and more than 80 ft (24 m) long, Barosaurus, a sauropod, was one of the biggest dinosaurs.

Barosaurus' tail was about 43 ft (13 m) long.

Compsognathus reached just below Barosaurus's ankle.

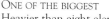

12

Compsognathus *had long
legs for running fast.*

*See the size of
Compsognathus compared
to Barosaurus at the
bottom of page 12.*

Barosaurus'
*extremely long neck
was balanced by its
very long tail.*

*Rows of
thick plates*

ONE OF THE SMALLEST
Fully grown when only 3 ft
(1m) long, Compsognathus,
a carnivore, was one
of the smallest
dinosaurs.

*Sharp spines
at the side*

WHAT ARE DINOSAURS?

DINOSAUR FACTS

• There were about
thirty times more
herbivores than
carnivores.

• The fastest dinosaurs
were the theropods,
which ran on two legs.

• Dinosaurs did not fly
or live in the sea.

• The sauropods were
the largest dinosaurs.

*Thick
legs*

SPIKY PROTECTION
The slow-moving ankylosaurs, which were
herbivores, had armored skin for protection from
sharp-toothed carnivores. *Edmontonia* had bony
plates and spikes on its skin. It lived at the same
time and in the same places as *Tyrannosaurus rex*,
so it needed all the protection its armor could give.

13

More types of dinosaur

We will never know how many different kinds of dinosaur existed over the 160 million years of their existence. We do know that some fossil remains belong not to the dinosaurs but to swimming and flying relatives.

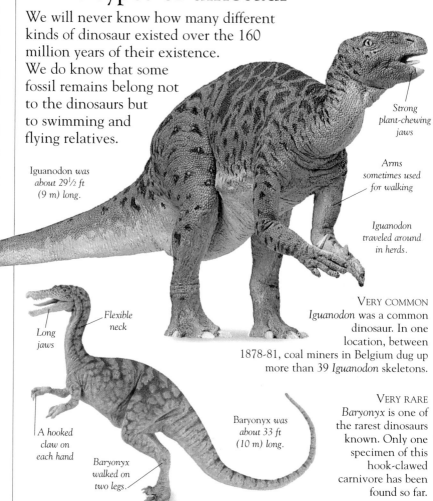

Strong plant-chewing jaws

Arms sometimes used for walking

Iguanodon was about 29½ ft (9 m) long.

Iguanodon traveled around in herds.

Flexible neck

Long jaws

A hooked claw on each hand

Baryonyx walked on two legs.

Baryonyx was about 33 ft (10 m) long.

VERY COMMON
Iguanodon was a common dinosaur. In one location, between 1878-81, coal miners in Belgium dug up more than 39 *Iguanodon* skeletons.

VERY RARE
Baryonyx is one of the rarest dinosaurs known. Only one specimen of this hook-clawed carnivore has been found so far.

14

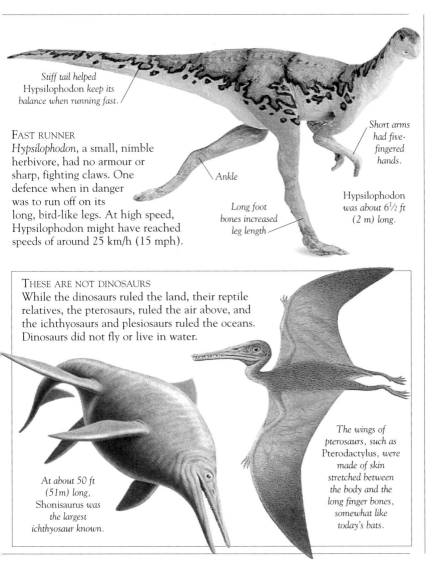

Stiff tail helped Hypsilophodon keep its balance when running fast.

SHORT ARMS had five-fingered hands.

FAST RUNNER
Hypsilophodon, a small, nimble herbivore, had no armour or sharp, fighting claws. One defence when in danger was to run off on its long, bird-like legs. At high speed, Hypsilophodon might have reached speeds of around 25 km/h (15 mph).

Ankle

Long foot bones increased leg length

Hypsilophodon was about 6½ ft (2 m) long.

THESE ARE NOT DINOSAURS
While the dinosaurs ruled the land, their reptile relatives, the pterosaurs, ruled the air above, and the ichthyosaurs and plesiosaurs ruled the oceans. Dinosaurs did not fly or live in water.

The wings of pterosaurs, such as Pterodactylus, *were made of skin stretched between the body and the long finger bones, somewhat like today's bats.*

At about 50 ft (51m) long, Shonisaurus *was the largest ichthyosaur known.*

DISCOVERING DINOSAURS

SIR RICHARD OWEN
(1804-92)

EVERYTHING WE KNOW about dinosaurs is based on their fossilized remains. These are pieced together to make the skeletons we see in museums. Sir Richard Owen, the famous dinosaur expert, first named some reptile fossils as dinosaurs in 1841.

Fossils

Fossils are the remains of ancient living things buried and preserved in rocks. Most fossils were formed from tough body parts, such as the bones of animals or the woody parts of plants. Fossilization is a very slow process – it usually takes millions of years.

SAUROPOD
TOOTH

TOUGH TOOTH
Worn surfaces on fossilized teeth show how different dinosaurs ate in different ways.

SAUROPOD
EGGSHELL
FRAGMENT

FOSSIL EGGSHELL
Dinosaur eggshells, such as this fragment from a sauropod egg, were hard enough to be preserved as fossils.

FOSSILIZED
CONES

OLD CONES
These pine cones from the Cretaceous period were tough enough to fossilize.

IGUANODON
CALF BONE

FOSSIL BONES
Sometimes when bones fossilize, slow chemical processes capture every detail of their original inner structure and outer shape. Even when bones are cracked and crushed, it is possible to identify scars where muscles were attached.

16

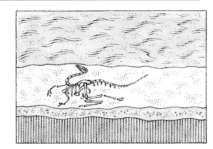

STORY OF A DINOSAUR FOSSIL

1 The dinosaur *Struthiomimus* lies dead on a riverbank. For *Struthiomimus* to have a chance of fossilization, it must be buried quickly before it rots away.

2 Buried under many layers of sediment, over millions of years, the hard parts of *Struthiomimus* change to stony fossils.

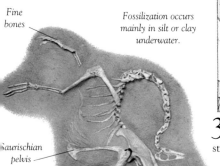

Fine bones

Fossilization occurs mainly in silt or clay underwater.

Saurischian pelvis

It is rare to find a perfectly preserved whole skeleton.

Long rear leg

3 Earth movements and erosion expose the skeleton at the surface. A scientist starts to chip away the surrounding rock.

UNCOVERED FOSSIL
An almost perfect fossil of *Struthiomimus*, lying in its death pose, has been carefully uncovered. Studying this skeleton gives scientists more clues in the dinosaur puzzle.

Preparing dinosaurs

MAKING A MOLD
To make a mold of an original bone, liquid rubber is painted on to the surface of the bone and left to set. When the rubber has set, it is removed from the bone in sections. It is then supported by cotton gauze and surrounded with a plastic jacket.

POURING THE MOLD
The inside of the rubber molds are painted with liquid plastic and strengthened by sheets of fiberglass. The mold sections are then joined together to recreate the bone's shape, and are filled with plastic foam.

Pouring the plastic foam into the bone cast

As scientists gain a better understanding of the way dinosaurs lived, museums try to arrange dinosaur skeletons in a variety of poses. Scientists at the American Museum of Natural History in New York built an exciting display. They showed a *Barosaurus* skeleton rearing up, defending its young against an attacking *Allosaurus*. Since the fossil bones of *Barosaurus* were very fragile and too heavy to display in such a pose, a lightweight replica of the skeleton was made.

Filing away the rough edges of the joins

FINISHING TOUCHES
The joins in the cast bones are smoothed by filing. The plastic bones are then painted to match the colours of the original bones.

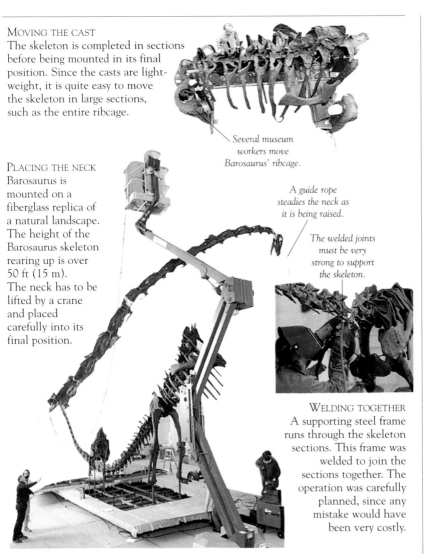

MOVING THE CAST

The skeleton is completed in sections before being mounted in its final position. Since the casts are lightweight, it is quite easy to move the skeleton in large sections, such as the entire ribcage.

Several museum workers move Barosaurus' ribcage.

PLACING THE NECK

Barosaurus is mounted on a fiberglass replica of a natural landscape. The height of the Barosaurus skeleton rearing up is over 50 ft (15 m). The neck has to be lifted by a crane and placed carefully into its final position.

A guide rope steadies the neck as it is being raised.

The welded joints must be very strong to support the skeleton.

WELDING TOGETHER

A supporting steel frame runs through the skeleton sections. This frame was welded to join the sections together. The operation was carefully planned, since any mistake would have been very costly.

STORING FOSSILS
The dinosaur fossils on display in museums are often just a fraction of the fossils the museum possesses. Sometimes thousands of fossils are housed in storerooms.

Dinosaurs on display

The most popular feature of many museums with natural history collections are the dinosaurs. Natural history museums around the world have dinosaur displays. Scientists use these museums for storing fossils, and as laboratories for studying dinosaurs and other fossils.

LIFE-SIZE SKELETON
Scientists and museum staff work together to construct a skeleton for display, such as this replica *Tyrannosaurus rex* skeleton. Full-size reconstructions of dinosaurs give us an impression of how they may have looked. This is particularly effective with awesome giants like *Tyrannosaurus*.

When running, Tyrannosaurus rex would have held its tail rigid for balance.

The back leg bones were thick to support Tyrannosaurus rex's enormous weight.

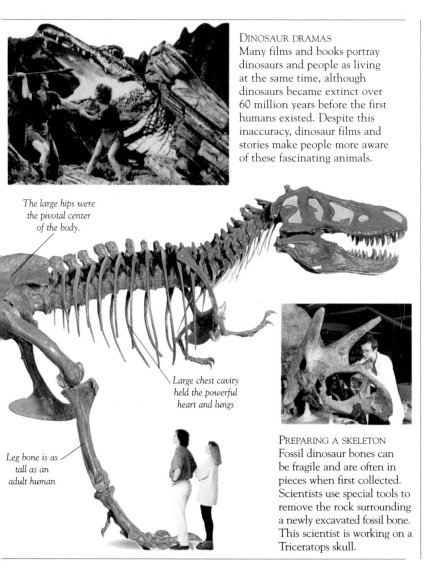

DINOSAUR DRAMAS
Many films and books portray
dinosaurs and people as living
at the same time, although
dinosaurs became extinct over
60 million years before the first
humans existed. Despite this
inaccuracy, dinosaur films and
stories make people more aware
of these fascinating animals.

*The large hips were
the pivotal center
of the body.*

*Large chest cavity
held the powerful
heart and lungs*

*Leg bone is as
tall as an
adult human*

PREPARING A SKELETON
Fossil dinosaur bones can
be fragile and are often in
pieces when first collected.
Scientists use special tools to
remove the rock surrounding
a newly excavated fossil bone.
This scientist is working on a
Triceratops skull.

DINOSAUR WORLD

THE WORLD HAS NOT always looked the way it does today. Continents are constantly moving, and this very gradually changes the appearance of the Earth. The Triassic, Jurassic, and Cretaceous worlds all looked very different from one another. Mountains grew up; erosion wore land away, and plants and animals, including the dinosaurs, appeared and disappeared.

Changing Earth

The Earth's lithosphere (outer layer) is made up of massive plates, which move on the semimolten rock underneath. Over millions of years plate movement has caused continents to join together and separate to produce the distribution of land today.

Two plates colliding forms mountain ranges

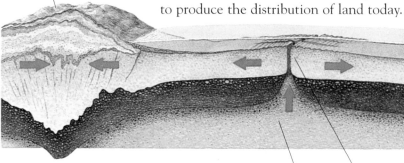

MOVING PLATES
As the plates move, they either collide, which sometimes forms mountain ranges, or they move apart, forming new crust. When plates move apart, molten mantle rock rises between them, cools, and adds to the Earth's crust.

The layer of semimolten rock beneath the lithosphere is called the mantle.

Molten mantle rock surfaces to form new crust.

Edge of plate

The constant movement of the plates is called continental drift.

WORLD MAP OF PLATES

PLATE BOUNDERIES
There are nine main plates and several smaller ones. The plates are in constant motion, moving at a rate of only a few inches each year.

TRIASSIC WORLD
In the Triassic period, when dinosaurs first appeared on Earth, all the land was joined together forming one gigantic continent. Scientists call this supercontinent Pangaea.

Land was joined together

Tethys Sea

Laurasia was made up of northern landmasses.

JURASSIC WORLD
In the Jurassic period, Pangaea gradually split into two continents. The continent in the north, made of large landmasses and smaller islands, is called Laurasia. The continent in the south is called Gondwanaland.

Gondwanaland

Sometimes when two plates meet, one slides beneath the other.

This landmass became South America.

CRETACEOUS WORLD
Toward the end of the Cretaceous period, the continents broke up into smaller landmasses. Plates collided, forming the Rocky Mountains in North America and other mountain ranges.

Triassic world

The Triassic period was the beginning of the Mesozoic era, which lasted until the end of the Cretaceous period. The first dinosaurs appeared in the Triassic period. These dinosaurs were agile carnivores that evolved rapidly. Some became herbivores. Small mammals also appeared at this time, as did the flying reptiles, called pterosaurs.

ORNITHOSUCHUS

COELOPHYSIS

PLANT LIFE
The biggest trees were conifers. These formed huge forests, together with cycads and ferns. Squat cycads and ferns were ground plants fed on by smaller animals.

CYCAD

CROCODILES

PLATEOSAURUS

LIFE IN THE AIR
The pterosaurs were cousins of the dinosaurs, and were the only reptiles ever to fly. They flew above the conifer forests catching insects. They may also have skimmed the water of the rivers and seas for fish.

This pterosaur, Preondactylus, *had a wingspan of about 5 ft (1.5 m).*

MELANOROSAURUS

DICYNODONTS

PLATEOSAURUS

HERRERASAURUS

DINOSAUR LIFE
The number of herbivores, such as *Plateosaurus*, increased during the Triassic period. They were stalked by carnivorous dinosaurs, such as *Herrerasaurus*. Other reptiles lived alongside the dinosaurs, such as the piglike dicynodonts.

Jurassic world

Early in the Jurassic period, the herbivorous dinosaurs were mainly prosauropods and small ornithopods. By the late Jurassic, herds of giant sauropods roamed the land. These dinosaurs, as well as other reptiles and mammals, fed on the lush plant life. The first birds appeared, but the pterosaurs remained the rulers of the skies.

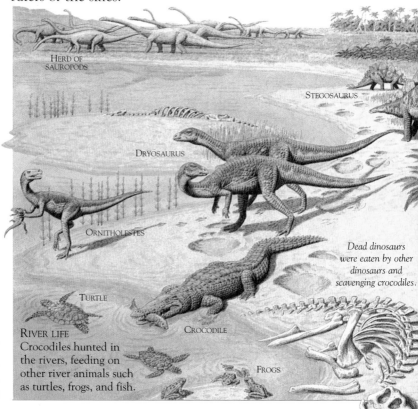

HERD OF SAUROPODS

STEGOSAURUS

DRYOSAURUS

ORNITHOLESTES

Dead dinosaurs were eaten by other dinosaurs and scavenging crocodiles.

TURTLE

CROCODILE

RIVER LIFE
Crocodiles hunted in the rivers, feeding on other river animals such as turtles, frogs, and fish.

FROGS

PLANT LIFE
Cycads, conifers, and ginkgoes dominated the forests. Ferns and horsetails provided a dense ground cover.

DINOSAUR LIFE
This was the age of the giant dinosaurs. Herds of *sauropods* marched across plains feeding on treetops. Fierce carnosaurs, such as *Allosaurus*, preyed on herbivores like *Stegosaurus*. Not all the dinosaurs were giants – tiny *Compsognathus* also lived in this period.

Cretaceous world

In the Cretaceous period, North America, Europe, and
Asia were part of a much larger continent called Laurasia.
Herbivorous dinosaurs, which included the ceratopsians and
the hadrosaurids, browsed among marshy lowlands. The
giant sauropods became rare. In the late Cretaceous
the terrifying tyrannosaurids appeared.
They were the top predators until
the extinction of the dinosaurs,
at the end of this period.

POLACANTHUS

CROCODILE

BARYONYX

CRICKET

BEETLE

DRAGONFLY

COCKROACH

DINOSAUR LIFE
Small herbivores were more common in
this period. Carnivores like *Baryonyx* may
have lived on fish, while tyrannosaurids
probably fed on other dinosaurs.

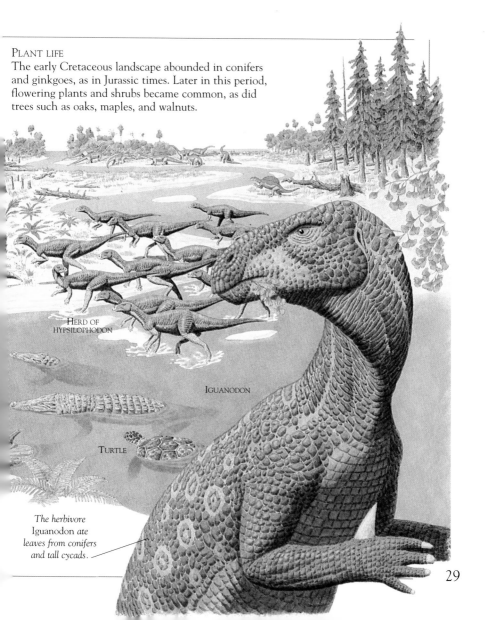

PLANT LIFE
The early Cretaceous landscape abounded in conifers and ginkgoes, as in Jurassic times. Later in this period, flowering plants and shrubs became common, as did trees such as oaks, maples, and walnuts.

HERD OF
HYPSILOPHODON

IGUANODON

TURTLE

The herbivore Iguanodon ate leaves from conifers and tall cycads.

29

Dinosaurs today

The remains of dinosaurs have been discovered on every continent, and new dinosaur fossils are constantly being discovered. They may be found by scientists on expeditions, by amateur fossil hunters, or by accident in places like building sites and underground mines. This map of the modern world shows the locations of the major dinosaur finds.

NORTH AMERICA
Expeditions are always being organized to search for dinosaurs in North America, since rocks from the dinosaur age are exposed over vast areas. The dinosaurs discovered here include:

- *Allosaurus*
- *Triceratops*
- *Deinonychus*
- *Camarasaurus*
- *Parasaurolophus*
- *Corythosaurus*
- *Stegosaurus*
- *Apatosaurus*
- *Coelophysis*

SOUTH AMERICA
Most South American dinosaurs have been found in Argentina and Brazil. Some of the earliest known dinosaurs have been found here. The South American dinosaurs include:

- *Saltasaurus*
- *Herrerasaurus*
- *Patagosaurus*
- *Staurikosaurus*
- *Piatnitzkyosaurus*

ANTARCTICA
The climate in Antarctica was much warmer in the dinosaur age than it is today. The bones of several small Cretaceous period dinosaurs have been found here, including a relative of the small ornithopod *Hypsilophodon*.

EUROPE

It was here in the 19th century that the first dinosaur fossils were collected and recorded, and where the name "dinosaur" was first used. Dinosaurs found in Europe include:

- Hypsilophodon
- Iguanodon
- Plateosaurus
- Baryonyx
- Compsognathus
- Eustreptospondylus

ASIA

Many exciting discoveries of dinosaurs have been made in the Gobi Desert. Scientists are still making new discoveries in China and India. Dinosaurs found in Asia include:

- Velociraptor
- Oviraptor
- Protoceratops
- Tuojiangosaurus
- Mamenchisaurus
- Gallimimus

AUSTRALIA AND NEW ZEALAND

There have been many fossil finds in Australia, and one in New Zealand. There are probably many sites rich in dinosaur fossils in these countries, but they have yet to be found. Dinosaurs found in these countries include:

- Muttaburrasaurus
- Leaellynosaura
- Austrosaurus
- Rhoetosaurus
- Minmi

AFRICA

Africa is a rich source of dinosaur fossils. A site in Tanzania has held some major discoveries. Dinosaurs found in Africa include:

- Spinosaurus
- Brachiosaurus
- Barosaurus
- Massospondylus

DINOSAUR ANATOMY

THE SIZE AND SHAPE of a dinosaur's head, body, and leg
help us to tell one dinosaur from another, and also tell
us how the body parts were used. From the skeleton
inside to the scaly skin outside, each part of a dinosaur
helps build a picture of these amazing animals.

Body power

The shoulder and pelvic muscles were crucial areas
of power for light, fast runners as well as slow,
heavy plodders. The largest
dinosaurs were not always
the mightiest. Some
of the smallest
dinosaurs were
powerful
runners.

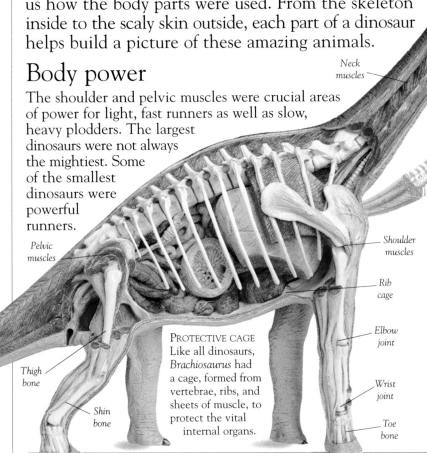

Neck muscles

Pelvic muscles

Shoulder muscles

Rib cage

Elbow joint

Thigh bone

Wrist joint

Shin bone

Toe bone

PROTECTIVE CAGE
Like all dinosaurs,
Brachiosaurus had
a cage, formed from
vertebrae, ribs, and
sheets of muscle, to
protect the vital
internal organs.

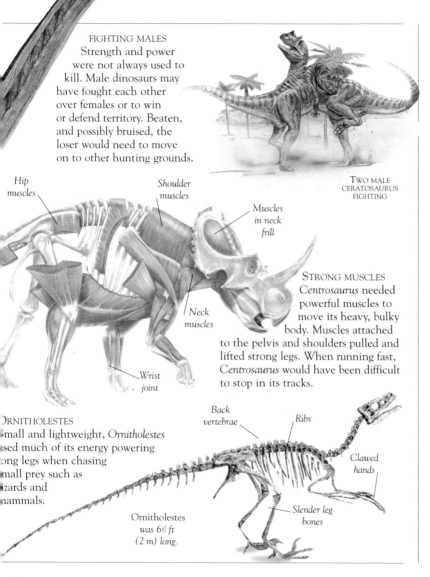

FIGHTING MALES

Strength and power were not always used to kill. Male dinosaurs may have fought each other over females or to win or defend territory. Beaten, and possibly bruised, the loser would need to move on to other hunting grounds.

TWO MALE
CERATOSAURUS
FIGHTING

Hip muscles

Shoulder muscles

Muscles in neck frill

Neck muscles

STRONG MUSCLES

Centrosaurus needed powerful muscles to move its heavy, bulky body. Muscles attached to the pelvis and shoulders pulled and lifted strong legs. When running fast, *Centrosaurus* would have been difficult to stop in its tracks.

Wrist joint

ORNITHOLESTES

Small and lightweight, *Ornitholestes* used much of its energy powering long legs when chasing small prey such as lizards and mammals.

Back vertebrae

Ribs

Clawed hands

Slender leg bones

Ornitholestes was 6½ ft (2 m) long.

Heads

Crests, frills, horns, and spikes adorned the heads of many dinosaurs. These decorations helped dinosaurs identify one another and were sometimes used for signaling. In a competition for territory, or control of a herd, the dinosaur with the most spectacular head might well have been the winner. Horned herbivores may have used their weapon for defense against hungry carnivores.

Large eye socket

Toothless jaws

BIRD BEAK
Gallimimus ate plants, insects, and lizards with its long, toothless beak. Its large-eyed skull looks very much like that of a big bird.

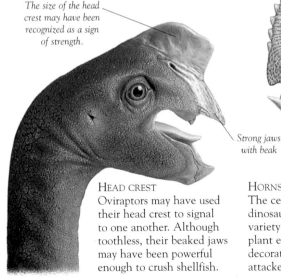

The size of the head crest may have been recognized as a sign of strength.

Strong jaws with beak

CENTROSAURUS HEAD

HEAD CREST
Oviraptors may have used their head crest to signal to one another. Although toothless, their beaked jaws may have been powerful enough to crush shellfish.

HORNS AND FRILLS
The ceratopsian group of dinosaurs had heads with a variety of frills and horns. These plant eaters probably used such decorations to frighten off attackers or to attract a mate.

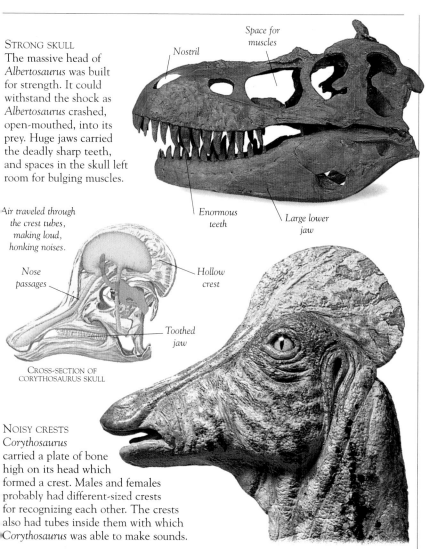

STRONG SKULL

The massive head of *Albertosaurus* was built for strength. It could withstand the shock as *Albertosaurus* crashed, open-mouthed, into its prey. Huge jaws carried the deadly sharp teeth, and spaces in the skull left room for bulging muscles.

Nostril

Space for muscles

Enormous teeth

Large lower jaw

Air traveled through the crest tubes, making loud, honking noises.

Nose passages

Hollow crest

Toothed jaw

CROSS-SECTION OF CORYTHOSAURUS SKULL

NOISY CRESTS

Corythosaurus carried a plate of bone high on its head which formed a crest. Males and females probably had different-sized crests for recognizing each other. The crests also had tubes inside them with which *Corythosaurus* was able to make sounds.

Necks

For dinosaurs, as with other animals, the neck was a vital channel between the head and body. Food passed from the mouth to the stomach through the neck; air was fed along the windpipe between the nostrils and lungs; nerves carried messages to and from the brain and body, and

BAROSAURUS
NECK VERTEBRA

blood traveled through arteries and veins. All of these lifelines, as well as powerful muscles, were supported on the framework of neck vertebrae (neck bones).

LONG AND FLEXIBLE
Herbivorous long-necked dinosaurs like *Barosaurus* probably used their flexible necks for cropping leaves from a large area of low-lying foliage while standing still. But if they needed to, they could have reached up to the leaves in tall trees.

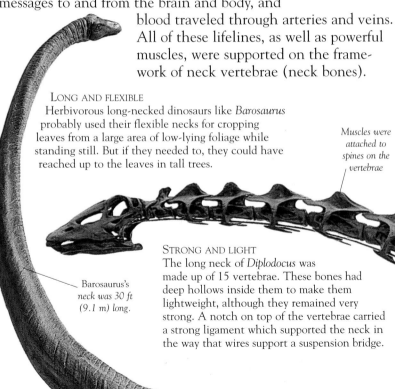

Muscles were attached to spines on the vertebrae

Barosaurus's
neck was 30 ft
(9.1 m) long.

STRONG AND LIGHT
The long neck of *Diplodocus* was made up of 15 vertebrae. These bones had deep hollows inside them to make them lightweight, although they remained very strong. A notch on top of the vertebrae carried a strong ligament which supported the neck in the way that wires support a suspension bridge.

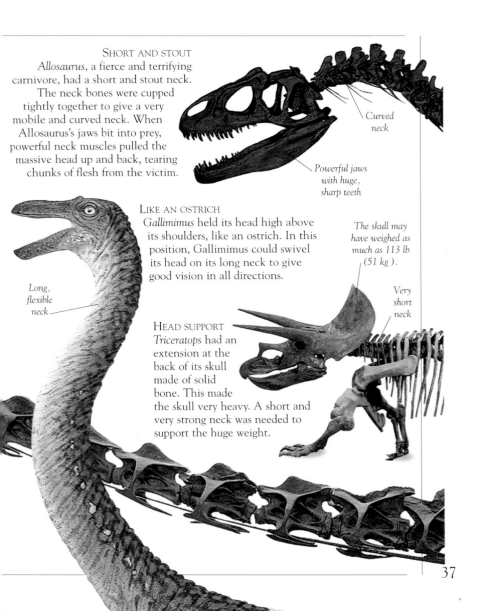

SHORT AND STOUT
Allosaurus, a fierce and terrifying carnivore, had a short and stout neck. The neck bones were cupped tightly together to give a very mobile and curved neck. When Allosaurus's jaws bit into prey, powerful neck muscles pulled the massive head up and back, tearing chunks of flesh from the victim.

Curved neck

Powerful jaws with huge, sharp teeth

LIKE AN OSTRICH
Gallimimus held its head high above its shoulders, like an ostrich. In this position, Gallimimus could swivel its head on its long neck to give good vision in all directions.

The skull may have weighed as much as 113 lb (51 kg).

Long, flexible neck

Very short neck

HEAD SUPPORT
Triceratops had an extension at the back of its skull made of solid bone. This made the skull very heavy. A short and very strong neck was needed to support the huge weight.

Dinosaur limbs

IGUANODON
FOOT BONE

Femur
(thigh bone)

Dinosaurs held their legs
directly beneath the body,
unlike other reptiles, which
crawl with their legs held out
from the sides of the body. Huge
herbivorous dinosaurs, such as
Diplodocus, walked on all fours with
front and rear legs supporting bulky bodies.
Most carnivores, such as *Albertosaurus*, walked
on the two back legs, leaving the front limbs
free for catching and holding prey.

Long,
slender
arms

Fingers have
8 in (26 cm)
claws

Three clawed
fingers on
each hand

MYSTERIOUS DINOSAUR
Almost all that is known of
Deinocheirus is this huge pair
of arms and hands. These
forelimbs are 8ft (2.4 m)
long. It is thought that
Deinocheirus belonged to
a group of dinosaurs called
ornithomimosaurs. The
huge hands would have
been used to catch
and hold prey.

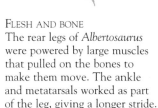

Knee

Muscle

Ankle

Metatarsals

Toe

FLESH AND BONE
The rear legs of *Albertosaurus*
were powered by large muscles
that pulled on the bones to
make them move. The ankle
and metatarsals worked as part
of the leg, giving a longer stride.

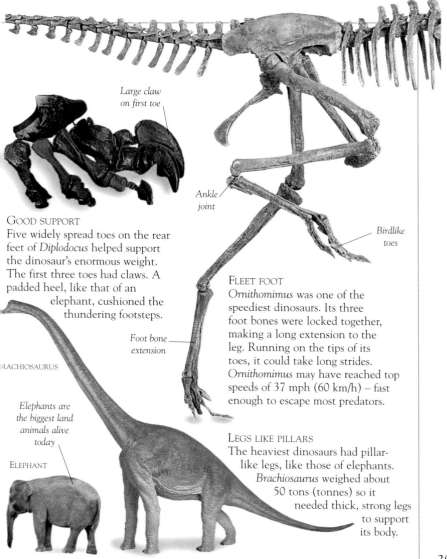

Large claw on first toe

Ankle joint

Birdlike toes

GOOD SUPPORT
Five widely spread toes on the rear feet of *Diplodocus* helped support the dinosaur's enormous weight. The first three toes had claws. A padded heel, like that of an elephant, cushioned the thundering footsteps.

Foot bone extension

BRACHIOSAURUS

Elephants are the biggest land animals alive today

ELEPHANT

FLEET FOOT
Ornithomimus was one of the speediest dinosaurs. Its three foot bones were locked together, making a long extension to the leg. Running on the tips of its toes, it could take long strides. *Ornithomimus* may have reached top speeds of 37 mph (60 km/h) – fast enough to escape most predators.

LEGS LIKE PILLARS
The heaviest dinosaurs had pillar-like legs, like those of elephants. *Brachiosaurus* weighed about 50 tons (tonnes) so it needed thick, strong legs to support its body.

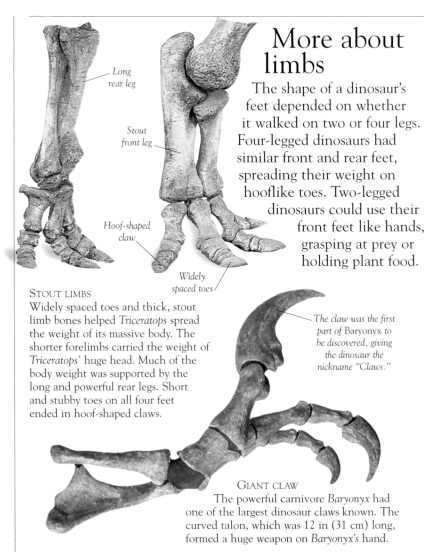

More about limbs

The shape of a dinosaur's feet depended on whether it walked on two or four legs. Four-legged dinosaurs had similar front and rear feet, spreading their weight on hooflike toes. Two-legged dinosaurs could use their front feet like hands, grasping at prey or holding plant food.

Long rear leg

Stout front leg

Hoof-shaped claw

Widely spaced toes

STOUT LIMBS
Widely spaced toes and thick, stout limb bones helped *Triceratops* spread the weight of its massive body. The shorter forelimbs carried the weight of *Triceratops'* huge head. Much of the body weight was supported by the long and powerful rear legs. Short and stubby toes on all four feet ended in hoof-shaped claws.

The claw was the first part of Baryonyx to be discovered, giving the dinosaur the nickname "Claws."

GIANT CLAW
The powerful carnivore *Baryonyx* had one of the largest dinosaur claws known. The curved talon, which was 12 in (31 cm) long, formed a huge weapon on *Baryonyx's* hand.

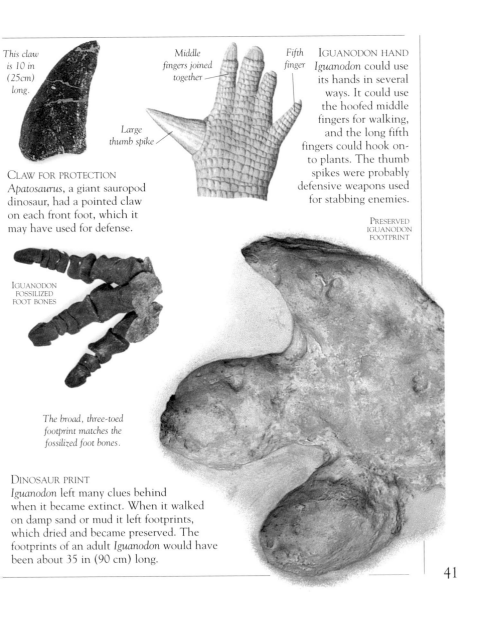

This claw is 10 in (25cm) long.

Middle fingers joined together

Large thumb spike

Fifth finger

IGUANODON HAND
Iguanodon could use its hands in several ways. It could use the hoofed middle fingers for walking, and the long fifth fingers could hook on-to plants. The thumb spikes were probably defensive weapons used for stabbing enemies.

CLAW FOR PROTECTION
Apatosaurus, a giant sauropod dinosaur, had a pointed claw on each front foot, which it may have used for defense.

PRESERVED
IGUANODON
FOOTPRINT

IGUANODON
FOSSILIZED
FOOT BONES

The broad, three-toed footprint matches the fossilized foot bones.

DINOSAUR PRINT
Iguanodon left many clues behind when it became extinct. When it walked on damp sand or mud it left footprints, which dried and became preserved. The footprints of an adult *Iguanodon* would have been about 35 in (90 cm) long.

41

Tails

Dinosaur tails had many uses, and tail bones can tell us a lot about their owners. Flexible tails ending with long, thin bones were the trademark of the giant sauropod dinosaurs. Dinosaurs that ran on two legs had tail bones that locked stiffly together to help give balance. Tails ending in lumps and spikes were used as weapons against attacking enemies.

Deinonychus could run very fast when chasing prey.

Tail bones tightly locked together

BALANCING ACT
Scientists once believed that *Parasaurolophus* used its thick tail for swimming by sweeping it from side to side like a fish's tail. But they now think that the tail counterbalanced the front of the body.

TAIL WHIP
When defending itself, *Diplodocus* used its long tail like a huge whip to swipe at its attacker. The tail had 73 bones joined together, and made a powerful weapon with its thin, whiplike ending.

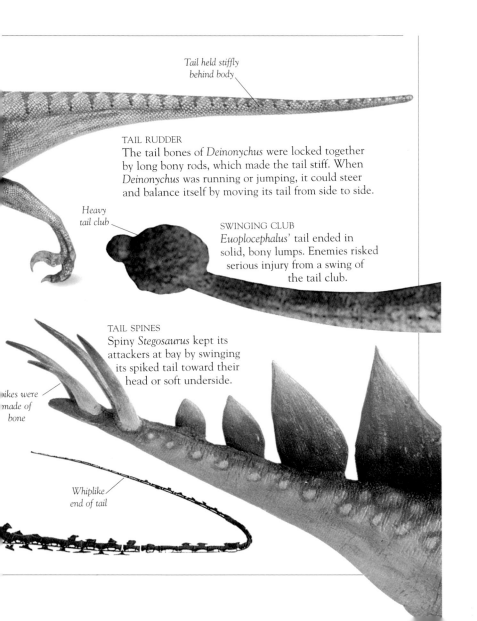

Tail held stiffly behind body

TAIL RUDDER
The tail bones of *Deinonychus* were locked together by long bony rods, which made the tail stiff. When *Deinonychus* was running or jumping, it could steer and balance itself by moving its tail from side to side.

Heavy tail club

SWINGING CLUB
Euoplocephalus' tail ended in solid, bony lumps. Enemies risked serious injury from a swing of the tail club.

TAIL SPINES
Spiny *Stegosaurus* kept its attackers at bay by swinging its spiked tail toward their head or soft underside.

Spikes were made of bone

Whiplike end of tail

SKIN SHAPE
Bony nodules, such as this one, were embedded in the skin of the armoured dinosaur *Polacanthus*.

Skin

Lizards and snakes, crocodiles and turtles – all have the tough scaly skin which is a trademark of reptiles. Dinosaurs were no exception. Their skin, preserved long enough in silt or clay to leave fossilized imprints, shows patterns of large and small lumps. Some dinosaurs, like the ankylosaurs, had spikes and plates of bone embedded in their thick skin – armour against attack from more dangerous dinosaurs.

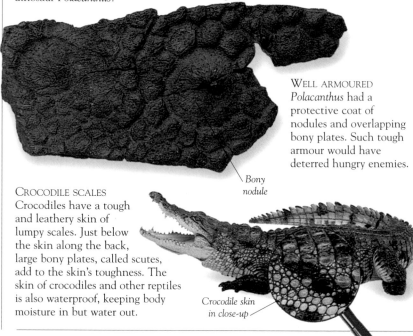

WELL ARMOURED
Polacanthus had a protective coat of nodules and overlapping bony plates. Such tough armour would have deterred hungry enemies.

Bony nodule

CROCODILE SCALES
Crocodiles have a tough and leathery skin of lumpy scales. Just below the skin along the back, large bony plates, called scutes, add to the skin's toughness. The skin of crocodiles and other reptiles is also waterproof, keeping body moisture in but water out.

Crocodile skin in close-up

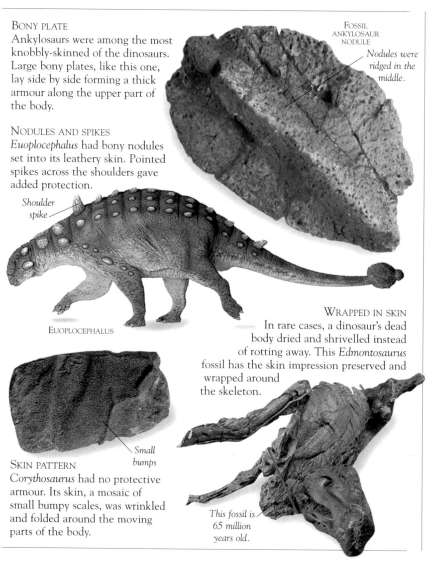

BONY PLATE

Ankylosaurs were among the most knobbly-skinned of the dinosaurs. Large bony plates, like this one, lay side by side forming a thick armour along the upper part of the body.

Nodules were ridged in the middle.

NODULES AND SPIKES

Euoplocephalus had bony nodules set into its leathery skin. Pointed spikes across the shoulders gave added protection.

Shoulder spike

EUOPLOCEPHALUS

WRAPPED IN SKIN

In rare cases, a dinosaur's dead body dried and shrivelled instead of rotting away. This *Edmontosaurus* fossil has the skin impression preserved and wrapped around the skeleton.

Small bumps

SKIN PATTERN

Corythosaurus had no protective armour. Its skin, a mosaic of small bumpy scales, was wrinkled and folded around the moving parts of the body.

This fossil is 65 million years old.

DINOSAUR LIFESTYLES

ALTHOUGH DINOSAURS died out 65 million years ago, we know a lot about their lifestyles. Herbivores and carnivores lived in the world of dinosaurs. Some dinosaurs cared for their young. But whether they were warm-or cold-blooded has yet to be established.

Carnivores

Most carnivores had deadly sharp teeth and claws. Some hunted in packs, some hunted alone, and others may have scavenged on dead animals which were possibly killed by disease.

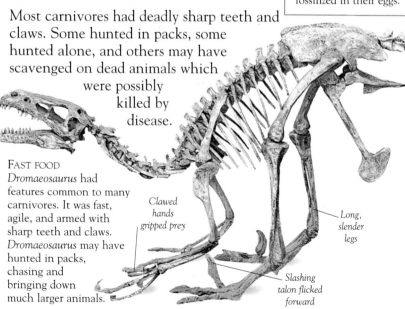

FAST FOOD
Dromaeosaurus had features common to many carnivores. It was fast, agile, and armed with sharp teeth and claws. *Dromaeosaurus* may have hunted in packs, chasing and bringing down much larger animals.

Clawed hands gripped prey

Long, slender legs

Slashing talon flicked forward

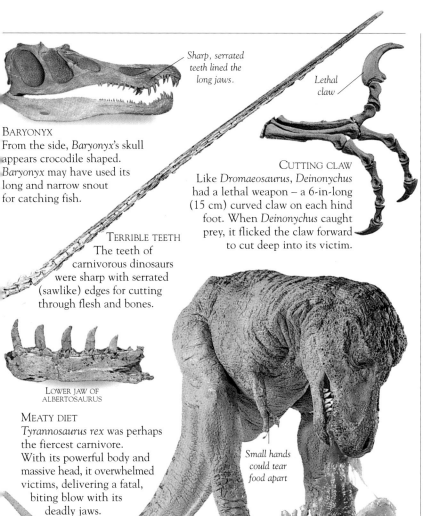

Sharp, serrated teeth lined the long jaws.

BARYONYX
From the side, *Baryonyx*'s skull appears crocodile shaped. *Baryonyx* may have used its long and narrow snout for catching fish.

Lethal claw

CUTTING CLAW
Like *Dromaeosaurus*, *Deinonychus* had a lethal weapon – a 6-in-long (15 cm) curved claw on each hind foot. When *Deinonychus* caught prey, it flicked the claw forward to cut deep into its victim.

TERRIBLE TEETH
The teeth of carnivorous dinosaurs were sharp with serrated (sawlike) edges for cutting through flesh and bones.

LOWER JAW OF ALBERTOSAURUS

MEATY DIET
Tyrannosaurus rex was perhaps the fiercest carnivore. With its powerful body and massive head, it overwhelmed victims, delivering a fatal, biting blow with its deadly jaws.

Small hands could tear food apart

Herbivores

Plant-eating dinosaurs had to eat large amounts of plants every day to fuel their bodies. An herbivore's special diet needed special ways of eating and digesting food. Some herbivores' teeth were shaped for chopping, raking, or crushing. Other herbivores had sharp beaks for snipping leaves and twigs. Once swallowed, these tough plants may have taken days to digest.

GRINDING GUT
Barosaurus did not chew its food – it swallowed tough leaves and twigs whole. In a part of its stomach, stones called gastroliths ground the food for digestion.

SMOOTH STONES
Gastroliths have been found near the skeletons of several dinosaurs.

HERBIVORE FACTS

• All ornithischian dinosaurs were herbivores.

• Some herbivores had up to 960 teeth.

• There were no flowers for dinosaurs to eat until about 125 million years ago.

• Herds of herbivores may have migrated during dry seasons to find fresh food supplies.

• Some of the plants the dinosaurs ate, such as pine trees, ferns, and cycads, still grow today.

48

PLANT PULP
Edmontosaurus had hundreds of tough teeth packed together in its upper and lower jaws. The two sets of teeth worked together like a pair of coarse files, grinding leaves, fruits, and seeds.

Lever for muscle attachment

EDMONTOSAURUS LOWER JAW

Toothless front of jaw

Serrated cutting edge

Teeth packed together

PARASAUROLOPHUS

Parasaurolophus feeding on a conifer.

Root of tooth

TOUGH TO EAT
We can see which plants were available to dinosaurs by studying plant fossils. Herbivores such as Parasaurolophus had strong teeth for chewing tough plants such as ferns and conifers.

LEAF CUTTERS
The teeth of sauropods such as Rebbachisaurus were designed for cutting rather than chewing.

MAGNOLIA

GINKGO

MONKEY PUZZLE CONIFER

DINOSAUR MENU
Many of the plants the dinosaurs ate can be seen in gardens and parks today.

Senses

Well-developed sight, smell, and hearing were crucial to the dinosaurs' long-running success. Dinosaurs used these vital senses daily for survival in their hostile world. Dinosaurs that were active hunters tracked prey by following noises and scents. Many dinosaurs lived in groups, and protected their young by listening and watching for predators.

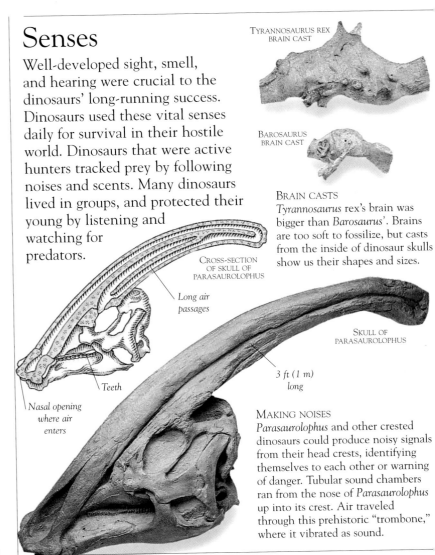

TYRANNOSAURUS REX
BRAIN CAST

BAROSAURUS
BRAIN CAST

BRAIN CASTS
Tyrannosaurus rex's brain was bigger than *Barosaurus*'. Brains are too soft to fossilize, but casts from the inside of dinosaur skulls show us their shapes and sizes.

CROSS-SECTION
OF SKULL OF
PARASAUROLOPHUS

Long air passages

Teeth

Nasal opening where air enters

SKULL OF
PARASAUROLOPHUS

3 ft (1 m) long

MAKING NOISES
Parasaurolophus and other crested dinosaurs could produce noisy signals from their head crests, identifying themselves to each other or warning of danger. Tubular sound chambers ran from the nose of *Parasaurolophus* up into its crest. Air traveled through this prehistoric "trombone," where it vibrated as sound.

50

COLOR

VIEW FROM LEFT   VIEW FROM RIGHT

BLACK AND WHITE

VIEW FROM LEFT   VIEW FROM RIGHT

DOUBLE VISION

We do not know if dinosaurs could see in color, but eye position affected the kind of image seen. Eyes on the sides of the head, common in herbivores, sent two different pictures to the brain.

COLOR

SINGLE VISION

Brain size is not always a sign of intelligence, but big-brained *Troodon* was probably one of the smartest dinosaurs. *Troodon* had large eyes and good vision. It benefitted from stereoscopic sight, which means it saw one image, the way that we do. Whether it could see in color or black and white, *Troodon* could judge distance when chasing or catching its prey.

BLACK AND WHITE

Warm and cold blood

Reptiles are cold-blooded, which means that they depend on conditions outside their body, such as the Sun's heat, for temperature control. Warm-blooded animals, such as mammals, produce heat from food energy, have hair for warmth, and sweat to cool down. Although dinosaurs were reptiles, much of their behavior, such as agile running, has more in common with mammals. Scientists are therefore puzzled over whether dinosaurs were warm- or cold-blooded.

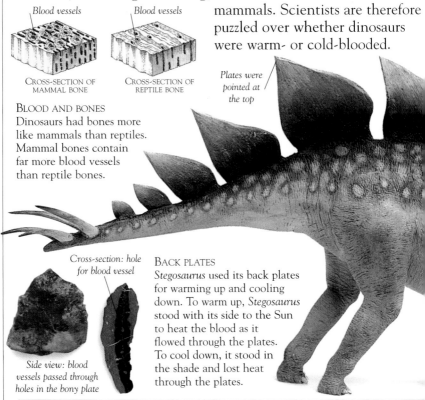

Blood vessels

CROSS-SECTION OF
MAMMAL BONE

Blood vessels

CROSS-SECTION OF
REPTILE BONE

Plates were pointed at the top

BLOOD AND BONES
Dinosaurs had bones more like mammals than reptiles. Mammal bones contain far more blood vessels than reptile bones.

Cross-section: hole for blood vessel

Side view: blood vessels passed through holes in the bony plate

BACK PLATES
Stegosaurus used its back plates for warming up and cooling down. To warm up, *Stegosaurus* stood with its side to the Sun to heat the blood as it flowed through the plates. To cool down, it stood in the shade and lost heat through the plates.

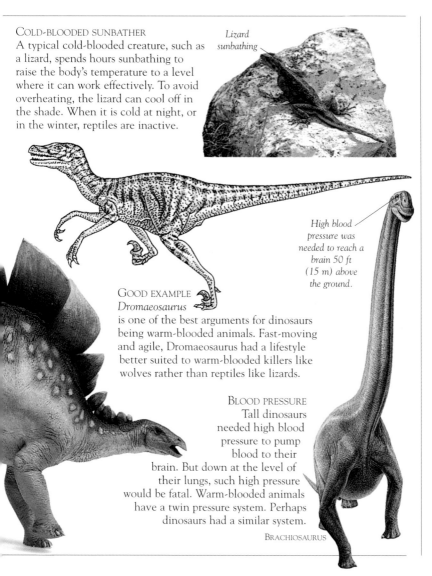

COLD-BLOODED SUNBATHER
A typical cold-blooded creature, such as a lizard, spends hours sunbathing to raise the body's temperature to a level where it can work effectively. To avoid overheating, the lizard can cool off in the shade. When it is cold at night, or in the winter, reptiles are inactive.

Lizard sunbathing

High blood pressure was needed to reach a brain 50 ft (15 m) above the ground.

GOOD EXAMPLE
Dromaeosaurus is one of the best arguments for dinosaurs being warm-blooded animals. Fast-moving and agile, Dromaeosaurus had a lifestyle better suited to warm-blooded killers like wolves rather than reptiles like lizards.

BLOOD PRESSURE
Tall dinosaurs needed high blood pressure to pump blood to their brain. But down at the level of their lungs, such high pressure would be fatal. Warm-blooded animals have a twin pressure system. Perhaps dinosaurs had a similar system.

BRACHIOSAURUS

Eggs, nests, and young

Dinosaurs laid eggs, like most other reptiles as well as birds. In recent years, scientists have discovered dinosaur nesting sites that gave them an insight into the early life of dinosaurs. These sites showed that some young stayed in their nests, cared for by adults, until they were old enough to leave. They also showed that dinosaurs, like many birds, used the same nesting sites year after year.

EGG FIND
The discovery of clutches of *Proto-ceratops* eggs was the first evidence that dinosaurs had nests. The shell of each egg had tiny air passages to permit gas exchange.

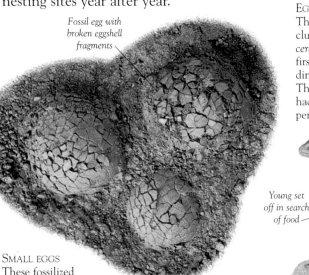

Fossil egg with broken eggshell fragments

Young set off in search of food

SMALL EGGS
These fossilized sauropod eggs, which are only 6 in (15 cm) in diameter, could have produced young that grew to an adult length of 39 ft (12 m). It probably took sauropods several years to reach their adult size.

HOME LIFE

Female *Maiasaura* laid about 25 eggs in a nest that was dug in the ground and lined with leaves and twigs. Young *Maiasaura* were about 12 in (30 cm) long when they hatched. They were reared in the nest until they grew to about 5 ft (1.5 m), when they would be old enough to start fending for themselves.

FOSSILIZED
MAIASAURA
EGG AND
SKELETON OF
YOUNG

Maiasaura hatchlings were very weak.

EARLY START

Unlike the *Maiasaura* young, who were looked after by their mother for several weeks, *Orodromeus* young left their nests as soon they hatched from their eggs. The young *Orodromeus* would have been preyed upon by carnivorous dinosaurs, such as sharp-sighted *Troodon*.

Newly hatched Orodromeus leaving nest

THE FIRST DINOSAURS

SEVERAL GROUPS of reptiles existed before the dinosaurs appeared. One group was the thecodonts. These were the ancestors of the dinosaurs, and they probably also gave rise to the pterosaurs and the crocodiles. Thecodonts were large carnivores that had straighter legs than other reptiles. The first dinosaurs were also carnivores, and the earliest known dinosaur, *Eoraptor*, first appeared 228 million years ago.

A VERY EARLY DINOSAUR *Eoraptor* may have been the first dinosaur. It was discovered in 1992 in Argentina. *Eoraptor* had a crocodile-like skull with sharp, curved teeth.

Jaws were lined with sharp teeth

Long, stiff tail

Long tail acted as a counterbalance to the front of the body

STAURIKOSAURUS

Staurikosaurus was about 6½ ft (2 m) long.

Long, birdlike back legs

STAURIKOSAURUS
Speedy *Staurikosaurus* was one of the first carnivorous dinosaurs. It had long, tooth-lined jaws for catching its prey, which it chased on its long and slender back legs.

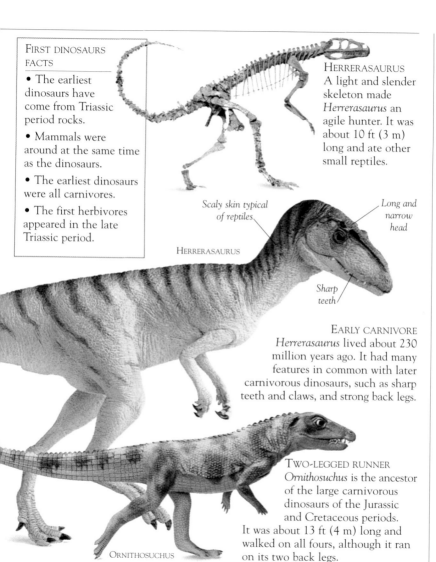

FIRST DINOSAURS FACTS

- The earliest dinosaurs have come from Triassic period rocks.

- Mammals were around at the same time as the dinosaurs.

- The earliest dinosaurs were all carnivores.

- The first herbivores appeared in the late Triassic period.

HERRERASAURUS
A light and slender skeleton made *Herrerasaurus* an agile hunter. It was about 10 ft (3 m) long and ate other small reptiles.

Scaly skin typical of reptiles

HERRERASAURUS

Long and narrow head

Sharp teeth

EARLY CARNIVORE
Herrerasaurus lived about 230 million years ago. It had many features in common with later carnivorous dinosaurs, such as sharp teeth and claws, and strong back legs.

TWO-LEGGED RUNNER
Ornithosuchus is the ancestor of the large carnivorous dinosaurs of the Jurassic and Cretaceous periods. It was about 13 ft (4 m) long and walked on all fours, although it ran on its two back legs.

ORNITHOSUCHUS

DINOSAUR EXTINCTION

AROUND 65 MILLION years ago, the dinosaurs became extinct. At the same time, other creatures, such as the sea and air reptiles, also died out. There are many theories for this extinction. But, as with so many facts about dinosaurs, no one really knows for sure what happened.

Even the mighty Tyrannosaurus rex could not survive extinction.

ASTEROID THEORY
At the end of the Cretaceous period a giant asteroid struck Earth. The impact resulted in a dust cloud which circled the globe, blocking out the sunlight and bringing cold, stormy weather.

SLOW DEATH
The dinosaurs died out gradually, perhaps over a period of several million years. *Tyrannosaurus rex* was one of the last dinosaurs to become extinct.

VOLCANO THEORY

Many volcanoes were active during the Cretaceous period. There were vast lava flows in the area that is now India. This would have poured huge amounts of carbon dioxide into the air, causing overheating, acid rain, and the destruction of the protective ozone layer.

MAGNOLIA

FLOWERS

Flowering plants may have contributed to the extinction of the dinosaurs. Many of these plants would have been poisonous, and any herbivorous dinosaur that ate them may have died. Many carnivores, which fed on herbivores, would then have died because of lack of food.

Crocodiles have not changed much in appearance over the years.

Megazostrodon *was a mammal that lived in the Triassic period.*

MAMMALS

Mammals appeared during the Triassic period, when they lived alongside the dinosaurs. They became the dominant land animals after the dinosaurs' extinction.

SURVIVING REPTILES

Crocodiles were around before the dinosaurs, and are still alive today. The reason these reptiles survived while the dinosaurs died out is a complete mystery.

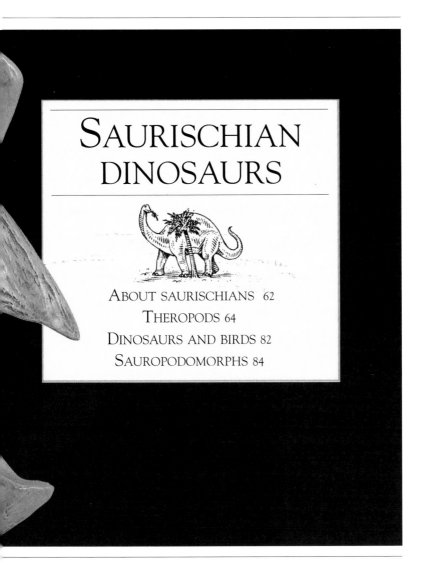

SAURISCHIAN DINOSAURS

ABOUT SAURISCHIANS

THERE WERE two main groups of saurischians – the theropods and the sauropodomorphs. The largest dinosaurs, and some of the smallest, were saurischians. This group differed from ornithischians mainly because of the shape of the hipbones.

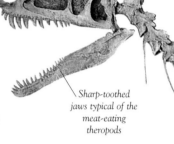

Sharp-toothed jaws typical of the meat-eating theropods

SAUROPODOMORPHS
Members of the sauropodomorph group were mainly herbivorous and quadrupedal (walked on four legs). The sauropodomorphs included the largest of all dinosaurs, *Seismosaurus*, which was about 130 ft (40 m) long.

TYRANNOSAURUS
REX

BAROSAURUS – A
SAUROPODOMORPH

THEROPODS
All theropods were carnivores, and were bipedal (walked on two legs only). One of the smallest dinosaurs, *Compsognathus*, and the largest land-based carnivore, *Tyrannosaurus rex*, belonged in the theropod group.

COMPSOGNATHUS

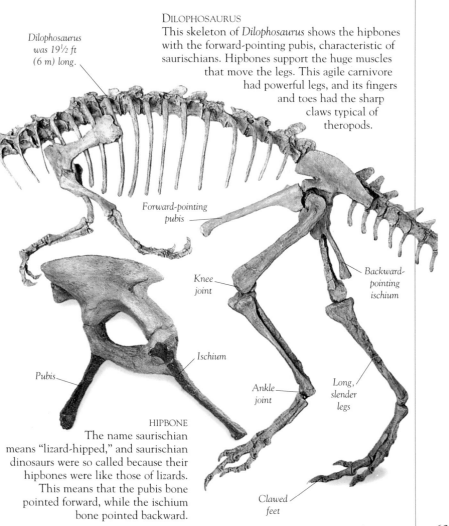

DILOPHOSAURUS

This skeleton of *Dilophosaurus* shows the hipbones with the forward-pointing pubis, characteristic of saurischians. Hipbones support the huge muscles that move the legs. This agile carnivore had powerful legs, and its fingers and toes had the sharp claws typical of theropods.

Dilophosaurus was 19½ ft (6 m) long.

Forward-pointing pubis

Knee joint

Backward-pointing ischium

Ischium

Pubis

Ankle joint

Long, slender legs

HIPBONE
The name saurischian means "lizard-hipped," and saurischian dinosaurs were so called because their hipbones were like those of lizards. This means that the pubis bone pointed forward, while the ischium bone pointed backward.

Clawed feet

THEROPODS

THE GROUP OF dinosaurs
called the theropods
were the killers of the dinosaur
world. Often large and ferocious,
these carnivores usually walked on
their two clawed rear feet. Theropod
means "beast feet," but their feet were
very birdlike. Each foot had three toes for
walking on, with long foot bones that added to
the length of the legs. Sharp-clawed hands were
often used for attacking and catching hold of prey.

EARLY THEROPOD
Dilophosaurus lived during
the early part of the Jurassic
period. An agile predator,
it was one of the first
large carnivorous
dinosaurs.

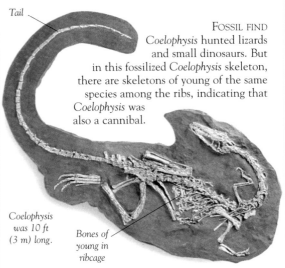

Tail

FOSSIL FIND
Coelophysis hunted lizards
and small dinosaurs. But
in this fossilized *Coelophysis* skeleton,
there are skeletons of young of the same
species among the ribs, indicating that
Coelophysis was
also a cannibal.

Coelophysis
was 10 ft
(3 m) long.

Bones of
young in
ribcage

THEROPOD FACTS

• All theropods were
carnivores.

• Coelophysis was
one of the first
theropods, living
about 220 million
years ago.

• Tyrannosaurus rex
was one of the last
theropods, living 65
million years ago.

• Many theropods
had no fourth or fifth
fingers.

• At least five
vertebrae supported
the pelvis of theropods.

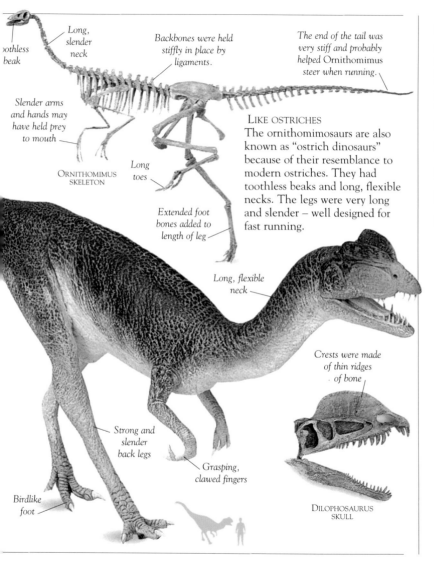

Toothless beak

Long, slender neck

Backbones were held stiffly in place by ligaments.

The end of the tail was very stiff and probably helped Ornithomimus steer when running.

Slender arms and hands may have held prey to mouth

ORNITHOMIMUS SKELETON

Long toes

Extended foot bones added to length of leg

LIKE OSTRICHES

The ornithomimosaurs are also known as "ostrich dinosaurs" because of their resemblance to modern ostriches. They had toothless beaks and long, flexible necks. The legs were very long and slender – well designed for fast running.

Long, flexible neck

Crests were made of thin ridges of bone

Strong and slender back legs

Grasping, clawed fingers

Birdlike foot

DILOPHOSAURUS SKULL

65

Carnosaurs

Of all the theropods, the ferocious carnosaurs are probably the most famous. Some carnosaurs could run as fast as 22 mph (35 km/h) on their large and powerful back legs. Massive heads carried a fearsome array of enormous serrated and curved teeth. *Tyrannosaurus rex* was the largest of the carnosaurs, and the most successful predator in the Cretaceous period. During the Jurassic, *Allosaurus* was the top predator.

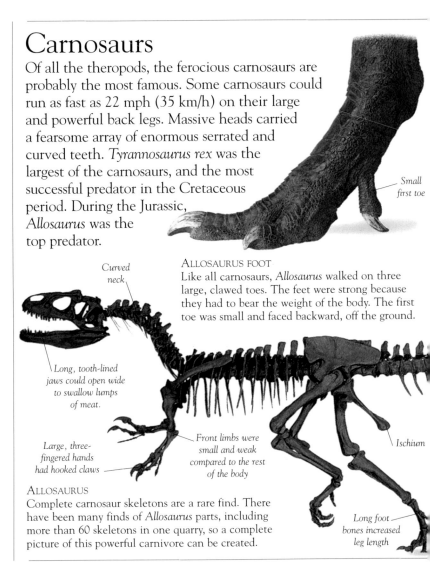

Small first toe

ALLOSAURUS FOOT
Like all carnosaurs, *Allosaurus* walked on three large, clawed toes. The feet were strong because they had to bear the weight of the body. The first toe was small and faced backward, off the ground.

Curved neck

Long, tooth-lined jaws could open wide to swallow lumps of meat.

Large, three-fingered hands had hooked claws

Front limbs were small and weak compared to the rest of the body

Ischium

Long foot bones increased leg length

ALLOSAURUS
Complete carnosaur skeletons are a rare find. There have been many finds of *Allosaurus* parts, including more than 60 skeletons in one quarry, so a complete picture of this powerful carnivore can be created.

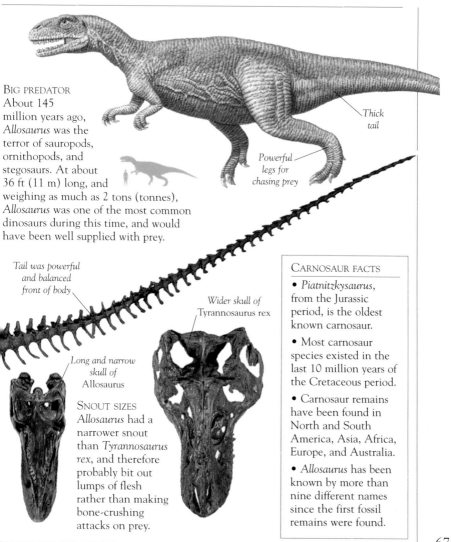

BIG PREDATOR
About 145 million years ago, *Allosaurus* was the terror of sauropods, ornithopods, and stegosaurs. At about 36 ft (11 m) long, and weighing as much as 2 tons (tonnes), *Allosaurus* was one of the most common dinosaurs during this time, and would have been well supplied with prey.

Thick tail

Powerful legs for chasing prey

Tail was powerful and balanced front of body

Wider skull of Tyrannosaurus rex

Long and narrow skull of Allosaurus

SNOUT SIZES
Allosaurus had a narrower snout than *Tyrannosaurus rex*, and therefore probably bit out lumps of flesh rather than making bone-crushing attacks on prey.

CARNOSAUR FACTS

• *Piatnitzkysaurus*, from the Jurassic period, is the oldest known carnosaur.

• Most carnosaur species existed in the last 10 million years of the Cretaceous period.

• Carnosaur remains have been found in North and South America, Asia, Africa, Europe, and Australia.

• *Allosaurus* has been known by more than nine different names since the first fossil remains were found.

CARNOTAURUS
HEAD

More carnosaurs

Fossilized remains of carnosaurs have been found worldwide. Many of the carnosaur skeletons that have been found are very incomplete. Consequently, they are difficult to study and understand, since pictures of whole dinosaurs have to be built up from small fragments of evidence. Scientists cannot even be sure that all of the dinosaurs they have grouped in the carnosaur group are, in fact, carnosaurs.

Tail held out to counterbalance front of body

SPINOSAURUS
A large sail of skin supported on long vertical spines ran along the back of *Spinosaurus*. This sail is thought to have acted as a heat regulator, like the back plates of *Stegosaurus*. The sail may also have been used for recognition between rivals, or to attract a mate.

The spines were up to 6 ft (1.8 m) in length.

Thick carnosaur tail

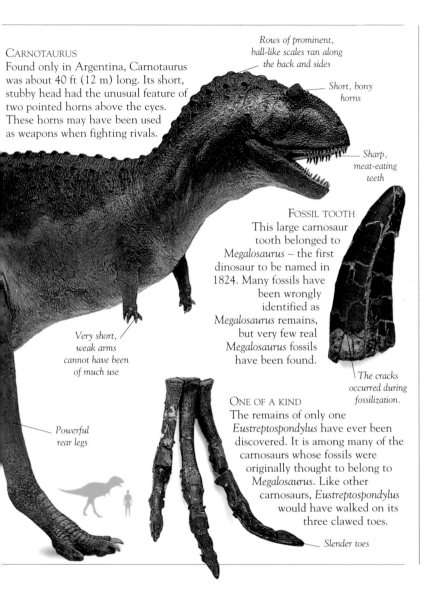

CARNOTAURUS

Found only in Argentina, Carnotaurus was about 40 ft (12 m) long. Its short, stubby head had the unusual feature of two pointed horns above the eyes. These horns may have been used as weapons when fighting rivals.

Rows of prominent, ball-like scales ran along the back and sides

Short, bony horns

Sharp, meat-eating teeth

Very short, weak arms cannot have been of much use

Powerful rear legs

FOSSIL TOOTH

This large carnosaur tooth belonged to *Megalosaurus* – the first dinosaur to be named in 1824. Many fossils have been wrongly identified as *Megalosaurus* remains, but very few real *Megalosaurus* fossils have been found.

The cracks occurred during fossilization.

ONE OF A KIND

The remains of only one *Eustreptospondylus* have ever been discovered. It is among many of the carnosaurs whose fossils were originally thought to belong to *Megalosaurus*. Like other carnosaurs, *Eustreptospondylus* would have walked on its three clawed toes.

Slender toes

Tyrannosaurids

Of all the carnosaurs, those in the tyrannosaurid family were the largest and probably the fiercest. The most famous member, *Tyrannosaurus rex*, was about 46 ft (14 m) long and 8 tons (tonnes) in weight. It is the largest land-based carnivore we know of. Tyrannosaurids not only caught and killed prey, they also scavenged dead creatures. They lived near the end of the Cretaceous period, and their remains have been found in North America and eastern Asia.

TYRANNOSAURUS REX TOOTH

Serrated edge

BIG TEETH
Tyrannosaurids had huge mouths, rimmed with huge, curved, serrated teeth. Some *Tyrannosaurus rex* teeth were 7 in (18 cm) long.

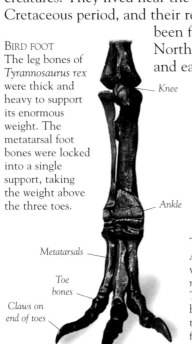

BIRD FOOT
The leg bones of *Tyrannosaurus rex* were thick and heavy to support its enormous weight. The metatarsal foot bones were locked into a single support, taking the weight above the three toes.

Knee

Tail raised for balance

Ankle

Metatarsals

Toe bones

Claws on end of toes

TYRANNOSAURUS REX
As the mightiest hunter, *Tyrannosaurus rex* would have had only another *Tyrannosaurus rex* to fear. But, like other animals, two *Tyrannosaurus rex* would have avoided confrontations, unless it was over females, territory, or food.

TERRIBLE TEETH
Daspletosaurus had the massive jaw typical of the tyrannosaurids, capable of delivering a deadly blow in one bite. Flesh and bones were sliced and crushed by the dagger-edged jaw.

This hungry Tyrannosaurus has spotted another Tyrannosaurus with a meal.

A loud roar warns intruder to stay away

A fight between two Tyrannosaurus would be a ferocious and bloody battle.

A weaker Tyrannosaurus might retreat rather than risk injury.

Clawed feet pin the food to the ground.

Ornithomimosaurs

With their toothless beaks and slender feet, the ornithomimosaurs looked like giant, featherless birds. But their ostrich-like appearance also had the dinosaur features of clawed hands and a long tail. Ornithomimosaurs were long-necked and large – up to 16 ft (5 m) long. They were among the fastest dinosaurs, racing on slim and powerful rear legs. A wide mouth enabled them to swallow sizable prey, such as small mammals, as well as insects and fruits.

ORNITHOMIMOSAUR FACTS

• The name ornithomimosaur means "bird-mimic reptile."

• Ornithomimosaurs may have ran as fast as 43 mph (70 km/h).

• Predators: carnosaurs and dromaeosaurs

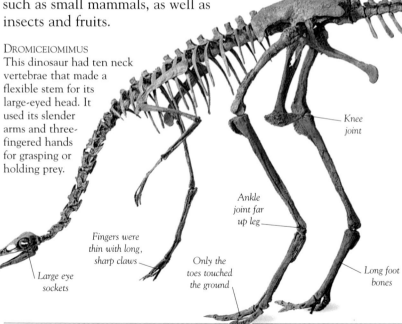

DROMICEIOMIMUS
This dinosaur had ten neck vertebrae that made a flexible stem for its large-eyed head. It used its slender arms and three-fingered hands for grasping or holding prey.

Knee joint

Ankle joint far up leg

Fingers were thin with long, sharp claws

Only the toes touched the ground

Long foot bones

Large eye sockets

LIKE AN OSTRICH *Struthiomimus* had a similar running style to an ostrich. But unlike an ostrich, *Struthiomimus* had long, mobile arms which helped its clawed fingers grasp and hold prey. Its long tail was an important balancer at high speed.

Ostrich speed – up to 50mph (80 km/h)

Struthiomimus speed – less than 30 mph (50 km/h)

Three locked foot bones

FOOT AND LEG
As in all other ornithomimosaurs, the feet and legs of *Dromiceiomimus* were built to give fast acceleration. Only the toes touched the ground – the foot bones were locked into a single, birdlike extension of the leg.

Sharp claws

Long, flexible neck

Mobile wrist

GALLIMIMUS
The largest ornithomimosaur was *Gallimimus*. It had a long and narrow, snouted head with large eyes for good sight. Its weak jaws were covered by a sharp, horny beak.

73

Oviraptosaurs

The first oviraptosaur to be discovered had a crushed skull and was lying on a nest of fossilized dinosaur eggs. The eggs belonged to an herbivore called *Protoceratops*. At the time of its death, the oviraptosaur was probably trying to steal the eggs to eat, and since its skull was crushed, it may have been caught and killed by an adult *Protoceratops*. Oviraptosaurs probably also ate berries and insects, as well as scavenging on the carcasses of dead animals.

FOSSILIZED NEST OF PROTOCERATOPS EGGS

STEALING EGGS
Nests of *Protoceratops* eggs may have been a favorite hunting ground for hungry oviraptosaurs.

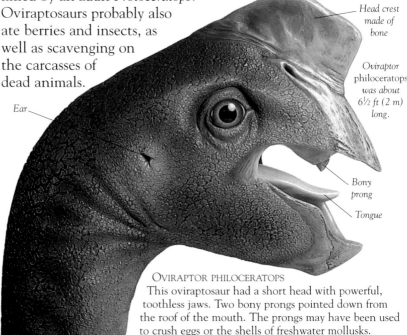

Head crest made of bone

Oviraptor philoceratops was about 6½ ft (2 m) long.

Ear

Bony prong

Tongue

OVIRAPTOR PHILOCERATOPS
This oviraptosaur had a short head with powerful, toothless jaws. Two bony prongs pointed down from the roof of the mouth. The prongs may have been used to crush eggs or the shells of freshwater mollusks.

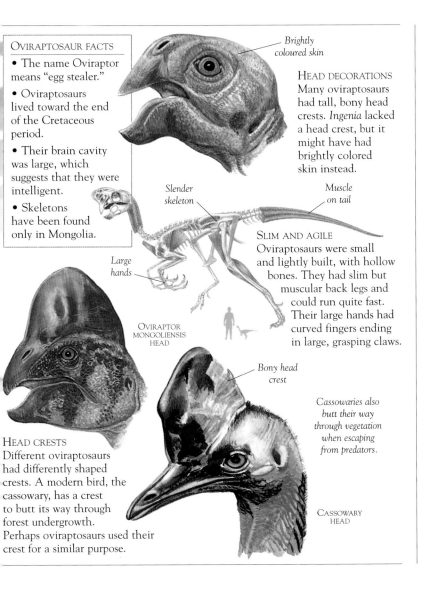

OVIRAPTOSAUR FACTS

• The name Oviraptor means "egg stealer."

• Oviraptosaurs lived toward the end of the Cretaceous period.

• Their brain cavity was large, which suggests that they were intelligent.

• Skeletons have been found only in Mongolia.

Brightly coloured skin

HEAD DECORATIONS
Many oviraptosaurs had tall, bony head crests. *Ingenia* lacked a head crest, but it might have had brightly colored skin instead.

Slender skeleton

Muscle on tail

SLIM AND AGILE
Oviraptosaurs were small and lightly built, with hollow bones. They had slim but muscular back legs and could run quite fast. Their large hands had curved fingers ending in large, grasping claws.

Large hands

OVIRAPTOR MONGOLIENSIS HEAD

Bony head crest

Cassowaries also butt their way through vegetation when escaping from predators.

HEAD CRESTS
Different oviraptosaurs had differently shaped crests. A modern bird, the cassowary, has a crest to butt its way through forest undergrowth. Perhaps oviraptosaurs used their crest for a similar purpose.

CASSOWARY HEAD

Troodontids

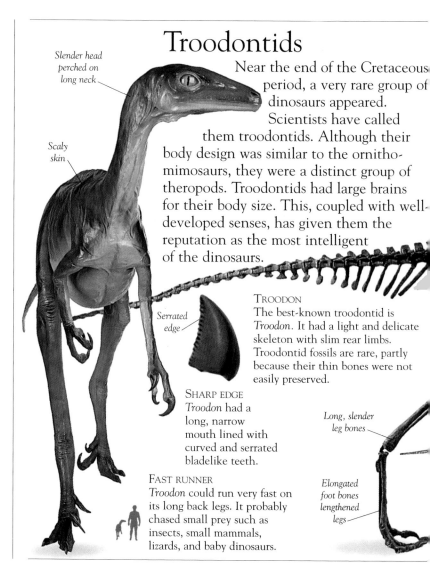

Near the end of the Cretaceous period, a very rare group of dinosaurs appeared. Scientists have called them troodontids. Although their body design was similar to the ornithomimosaurs, they were a distinct group of theropods. Troodontids had large brains for their body size. This, coupled with well-developed senses, has given them the reputation as the most intelligent of the dinosaurs.

Slender head perched on long neck

Scaly skin

Serrated edge

TROODON

The best-known troodontid is *Troodon*. It had a light and delicate skeleton with slim rear limbs. Troodontid fossils are rare, partly because their thin bones were not easily preserved.

SHARP EDGE

Troodon had a long, narrow mouth lined with curved and serrated bladelike teeth.

FAST RUNNER

Troodon could run very fast on its long back legs. It probably chased small prey such as insects, small mammals, lizards, and baby dinosaurs.

Long, slender leg bones

Elongated foot bones lengthened legs

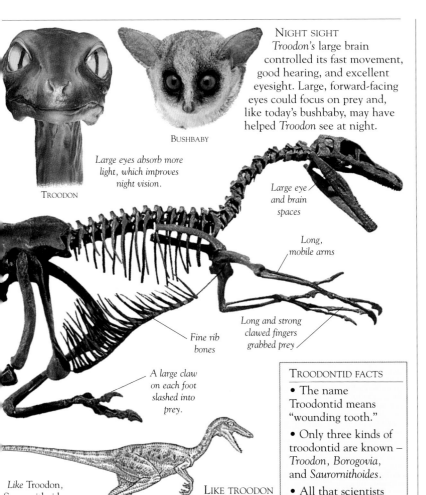

NIGHT SIGHT

Troodon's large brain controlled its fast movement, good hearing, and excellent eyesight. Large, forward-facing eyes could focus on prey and, like today's bushbaby, may have helped *Troodon* see at night.

BUSHBABY

Large eyes absorb more light, which improves night vision.

TROODON

Large eye and brain spaces

Long, mobile arms

Fine rib bones

Long and strong clawed fingers grabbed prey

A large claw on each foot slashed into prey.

Like Troodon, *Saurornithoides was a fast runner.*

LIKE TROODON

Saurornithoides was very similar to *Troodon*. It has been found only in Mongolia.

TROODONTID FACTS

• The name Troodontid means "wounding tooth."

• Only three kinds of troodontid are known – *Troodon, Borogovia,* and *Saurornithoides.*

• All that scientists knew of *Troodon* for several years was a single tooth.

77

Dromaeosaurids

These razor-toothed carnivores were very agile and had large brains and huge eyes with stereoscopic vision. They were among the most terrifying of all dinosaurs. A large sickle-shaped talon on their inner toes could rotate through 180°, slicing into their prey's tough hide.

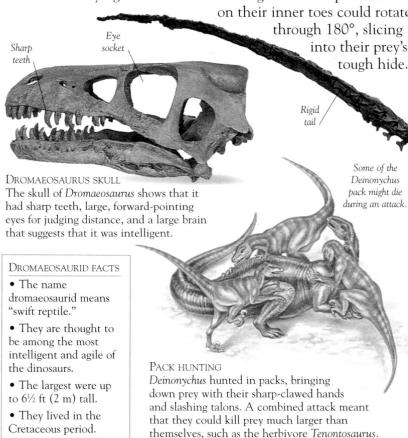

Sharp teeth

Eye socket

Rigid tail

Some of the Deinonychus pack might die during an attack.

DROMAEOSAURUS SKULL
The skull of *Dromaeosaurus* shows that it had sharp teeth, large, forward-pointing eyes for judging distance, and a large brain that suggests that it was intelligent.

DROMAEOSAURID FACTS

• The name dromaeosaurid means "swift reptile."

• They are thought to be among the most intelligent and agile of the dinosaurs.

• The largest were up to 6½ ft (2 m) tall.

• They lived in the Cretaceous period.

PACK HUNTING
Deinonychus hunted in packs, bringing down prey with their sharp-clawed hands and slashing talons. A combined attack meant that they could kill prey much larger than themselves, such as the herbivore *Tenontosaurus*.

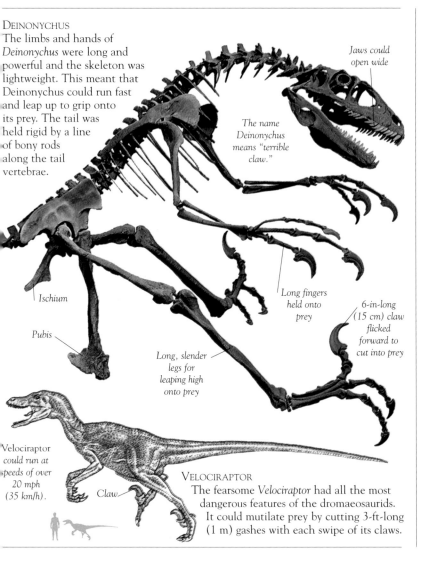

DEINONYCHUS
The limbs and hands of *Deinonychus* were long and powerful and the skeleton was lightweight. This meant that Deinonychus could run fast and leap up to grip onto its prey. The tail was held rigid by a line of bony rods along the tail vertebrae.

Jaws could open wide

The name Deinonychus means "terrible claw."

Ischium

Pubis

Long fingers held onto prey

6-in-long (15 cm) claw flicked forward to cut into prey

Long, slender legs for leaping high onto prey

Velociraptor could run at speeds of over 20 mph (35 km/h).

Claw

VELOCIRAPTOR
The fearsome *Velociraptor* had all the most dangerous features of the dromaeosaurids. It could mutilate prey by cutting 3-ft-long (1 m) gashes with each swipe of its claws.

Other theropods

COMPSOGNATHUS
SKULL

There was a huge variety of theropods. Most have been put into groups, like the carnosaurs, but some theropods, such as *Baryonyx*, *Ornitholestes*, and *Compsognathus*, do not fit into any of the established groups.

Baryonyx had an unusual, crocodile-like jaw, and a savage claw on each hand. *Compsognathus* and *Ornitholestes* were two of the smallest dinosaurs.

LIGHTWEIGHT HEAD
Chicken-sized *Compsognathus* had a small, pointed head with sharp, daggerlike teeth. The skull was lightly built and had huge openings, especially those of the orbits (eye sockets).

Curved, pointed teeth

SMALL AND FAST
Ornitholestes was swift and agile and may have hunted in packs. It grasped prey, such as small lizards and mammals, firmly between sharp thumb and finger claws.

Ornitholestes was about 6½ ft (2 m) long.

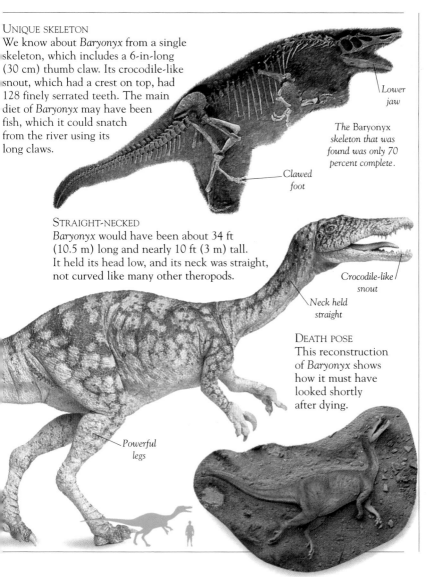

UNIQUE SKELETON

We know about *Baryonyx* from a single skeleton, which includes a 6-in-long (30 cm) thumb claw. Its crocodile-like snout, which had a crest on top, had 128 finely serrated teeth. The main diet of *Baryonyx* may have been fish, which it could snatch from the river using its long claws.

Lower jaw

The Baryonyx *skeleton that was found was only 70 percent complete.*

Clawed foot

STRAIGHT-NECKED

Baryonyx would have been about 34 ft (10.5 m) long and nearly 10 ft (3 m) tall. It held its head low, and its neck was straight, not curved like many other theropods.

Crocodile-like snout

Neck held straight

DEATH POSE

This reconstruction of *Baryonyx* shows how it must have looked shortly after dying.

Powerful legs

DINOSAURS AND BIRDS

SURPRISING THOUGH it might seem, scientists now recognize birds as the closest living relatives of dinosaurs. The most primitive bird is *Archaeopteryx*. In 1861, an *Archaeopteryx* skeleton together with fossil impressions of its feathers were found in a quarry in Germany. *Archaeopteryx* lived about 140 million years ago, alongside the dinosaurs that it resembled in many ways.

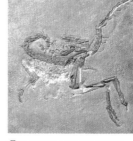

COMPSOGNATHUS FOSSIL
The fossil skeletons of *Compsognathus* (above) and *Archaeopteryx* look very similar. Scientists found an *Archaeopteryx* skeleton in 1951, but for 22 years they mistakenly thought it was a *Compsognathus* skeleton.

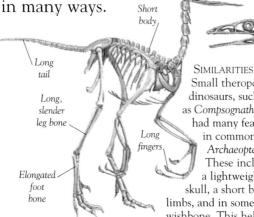

Lightweight skull

Short body

Long tail

Long, slender leg bone

Long fingers

Elongated foot bone

ARCHAEOPTERYX SKELETON

COMPSOGNATHUS SKELETON

Long tail

Short body

SIMILARITIES
Small theropod dinosaurs, such as *Compsognathus*, had many features in common with *Archaeopteryx*. These included a lightweight skull, a short body, long, thin limbs, and in some theropods, a wishbone. This helps confirm their close relationship.

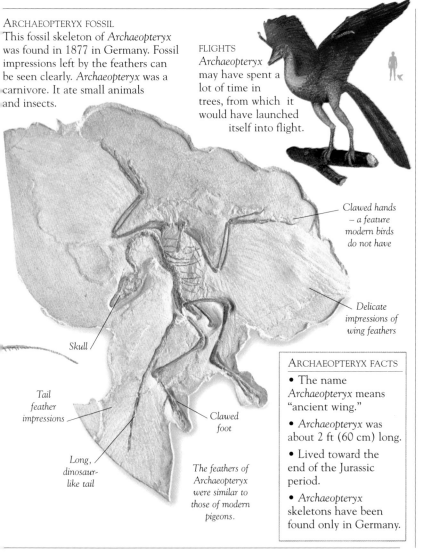

ARCHAEOPTERYX FOSSIL
This fossil skeleton of *Archaeopteryx* was found in 1877 in Germany. Fossil impressions left by the feathers can be seen clearly. *Archaeopteryx* was a carnivore. It ate small animals and insects.

FLIGHTS
Archaeopteryx may have spent a lot of time in trees, from which it would have launched itself into flight.

Clawed hands – a feature modern birds do not have

Delicate impressions of wing feathers

Skull

Tail feather impressions

Long, dinosaur-like tail

Clawed foot

The feathers of *Archaeopteryx* were similar to those of modern pigeons.

ARCHAEOPTERYX FACTS

• The name *Archaeopteryx* means "ancient wing."

• *Archaeopteryx* was about 2 ft (60 cm) long.

• Lived toward the end of the Jurassic period.

• *Archaeopteryx* skeletons have been found only in Germany.

SAUROPODOMORPHS

TWO GROUPS, the prosauropods and the sauropods, are included in the sauropodomorphs. Unlike the theropods, most sauropodomorphs were quadrupedal (walked on four legs) and were herbivores. They had long necks and tails, and ranged in size from 6½ ft (2 m) to 130 ft (40 m) in length.

APATOSAURUS
THUMB CLAW

THUMB CLAW
Many sauropodomorphs had big, curved thumb claws. They probably used these dangerous weapons for defense.

Long, flexible neck

Large front feet could hold plants when feeding

Plateosaurus may have often walked on only two legs.

Prosauropods such as Plateosaurus were the first large land animals.

PLATEOSAURUS
Several complete skeletons of the prosauropod *Plateosaurus* have been found. It is one of the earliest and largest saurischian dinosaurs of the Triassic period. Although quadrupedal, it could probably stand on its hind legs to reach up to feed on the higher branches.

Small skull

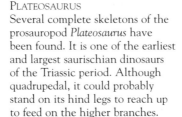

Tail was held off the ground when walking

BAROSAURUS SKULL

Sauropods, such as Barosaurus, had no molars or grinding teeth for chewing. Their food was probably ground by pebbles in their gizzards after being swallowed whole.

Teeth raked in food

BAROSAURUS SKULL

BRACHIOSAURUS

One of the largest land animals that we know of, Brachiosaurus could weigh over 68 tons (tonnes). Reaching 40 ft (12 m) in height it could eat from the tops of the tallest trees.

Long neck

STRONG SUPPORT

Brachiosaurus' dorsal (back) vertebrae had to be extremely strong to support its enormous weight.

Thick legs supported heavy weight

Front legs were longer than back legs

SAUROPODOMORPH FACTS

• The name sauropodomorph means "lizard-footed forms."

• The largest dinosaur was a sauropod called *Seismosaurus*.

• All sauropodomorphs were herbivores, although some may have eaten meat as well.

Prosauropods

The *prosauropods* are thought to be the ancestors of the sauropods. Both groups have long necks and small heads, but the prosauropods were generally smaller in size. Most prosauropods were herbivores, although some may have been omnivores (eating both meat and plants).

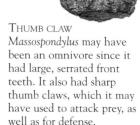

MASSOSPONDYLUS THUMB CLAW

THUMB CLAW
Massospondylus may have been an omnivore since it had large, serrated front teeth. It also had sharp thumb claws, which it may have used to attack prey, as well as for defense.

Teeth

Eye socket

SMALL SKULL
Riojasaurus, at 33 ft (10 m) in length, was the largest prosauropod. As with other prosauropods, its skull was tiny compared to its massive body, and its jaws were lined with leaf-shaped teeth for shredding plant food.

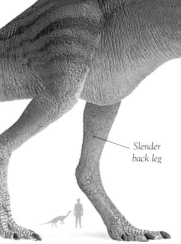

ANCHISAURUS
This prosauropod was designed to walk on all fours, but it may have occasionally run on two feet. *Anchisaurus* had large, sickle-shaped thumb claws which would have been dangerous weapons against attackers.

Slender back leg

PROSAUROPOD FACTS
• The name prosauropod means "before sauropods."

• All prosauropods had small heads, long necks, and long tails.

• *Plateosaurus* was the first large dinosaur.

• Their remains have been found worldwide, except Antarctica.

VIEW FROM ABOVE
This view from above of *Anchisaurus* shows that its body was long and slender. It would have held its tail off the ground when walking.

Slim and flexible neck

REACHING HIGH
Plateosaurus was one of the earliest and largest saurischian dinosaurs. It grew to about 26 ft (8 m) in length, and could stand on its hind legs to reach tall trees when feeding.

Lower arm

Large thumb claw

Thumb claw

PULLING CLAW
The toes on the hands of *Plateosaurus* varied greatly in length. The thumb, the largest, ended with a huge, sharp claw.

87

Sauropods

The largest-ever land animals were included in the sauropod group. Sauropods were quadrupedal, plant-eating saurischian dinosaurs. They all had huge bodies with long necks and elephant-like legs. They also had long tails which they used as whiplike weapons against enemies.

TAIL REINFORCEMENT
Tail bones like the one above were on the underside of *Diplodocus'* tail. They reinforced and protected the tail when it was pressed against the ground.

FRONT TEETH
Diplodocus had a long skull with peglike teeth at the front of the jaws. The teeth would have raked in plants such as cycads, ginkgoes, and conifers. *Diplodocus* had no back teeth for chewing, so the food was probably ground in the stomach by gastroliths (stomach stones).

Peglike teeth

Back of jaws was toothless

APATASAURUS
This sauropod was once known as Brontosaurus. At 73 ft (23 m) long and weighing 27 tons (tonnes), it was one of the largest sauropods. It had a long, horselike head with a fist-sized brain, and powerful legs with padded feet.

Tail contain 82 bon

TAIL WEAPON
Barosaurus resembled *Diplodocus*, but had a slightly longer neck and a shorter tail. The narrow tail may have been a defense weapon.

Tail may have been used like a whip against enemies

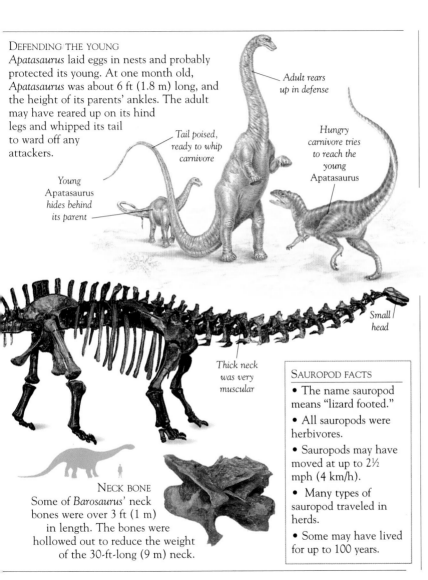

DEFENDING THE YOUNG

Apatasaurus laid eggs in nests and probably protected its young. At one month old, *Apatasaurus* was about 6 ft (1.8 m) long, and the height of its parents' ankles. The adult may have reared up on its hind legs and whipped its tail to ward off any attackers.

Adult rears up in defense

Hungry carnivore tries to reach the young Apatasaurus

Tail poised, ready to whip carnivore

Young Apatasaurus hides behind its parent

Small head

Thick neck was very muscular

NECK BONE
Some of *Barosaurus'* neck bones were over 3 ft (1 m) in length. The bones were hollowed out to reduce the weight of the 30-ft-long (9 m) neck.

SAUROPOD FACTS
• The name sauropod means "lizard footed."

• All sauropods were herbivores.

• Sauropods may have moved at up to 2½ mph (4 km/h).

• Many types of sauropod traveled in herds.

• Some may have lived for up to 100 years.

More sauropods

Scientists used to think that the ankylosaurs were the only armored dinosaurs. But the discovery of *Saltasaurus* proved that some sauropods had armor, too. It was also thought that sauropods may have lived in water, but we now know that the high water pressure at depth would not have allowed them to breathe.

SHORT SKULL
The short and high skull of *Camarasaurus* has a very large orbit (eye socket) and naris (nostril socket). There are approximately 48 spoonlike teeth.

Toothless snout tugged leaves from trees

SALTASAURUS
At 39 ft (12 m) long, *Saltasaurus* was quite small for a sauropod. Its armor consisted of large bony plates surrounded by smaller bony nodules. The armor possibly covered *Saltasaurus'* back and sides. The group of armored sauropods is called the titanosaurids.

SEGNOSAURUS
This sauropod was an unusual dinosaur. It does not look like a sauropodomorph, and some scientists place it in a group by itself. Although *Segnosaurus* ate plants, it may also have eaten meat. Its hands had long, curved claws which it may have used to scratch at termite mounds.

Segnosaurus
at termite mound

CETIOSAURUS
An early sauropod, *Cetiosaurus* had massive, heavy, and solid. Later sauropods had bones that were light and hollow.

Cetiosaurus was the first sauropod to be discovered.

Cetiosaurus may have weighed as much as five elephants.

Thick legs to support enormous weight

Bony nodules

NODULES
Only randomly scattered nodules of *Saltasaurus* have been found, so we can only guess at their position on its body.

Bony lumps

SKIN IMPRESSION
Parts of the body of *Saltasaurus* were protected by a covering of tightly packed, pea-sized, bony lumps.

ORNITHISCHIAN DINOSAURS

ABOUT ORNITHISCHIANS

THERE WERE FIVE main groups of ornithischians. They were all herbivores with hoofed feet and hipbones arranged like modern birds. They also had beaked mouths, apart from those in the pachycephalosaur group. Ornithischians were either bipedal or quadrupedal. Bipedal ornithischians had stiffened tails to counterbalance their bodies while feeding or running.

CERATOPSIANS

ANKYLOSAURS

ORNITHOPODS

PACHYCEPHALOSAURS

FIVE GROUPS
The five groups of ornithischians were: ceratopsians, with their neck frills; ankylosaurs, with their body armor; pachycephalosaurs, with their domed heads; stegosaurs, with their back plates, and the birdlike ornithopods.

STEGOSAURS

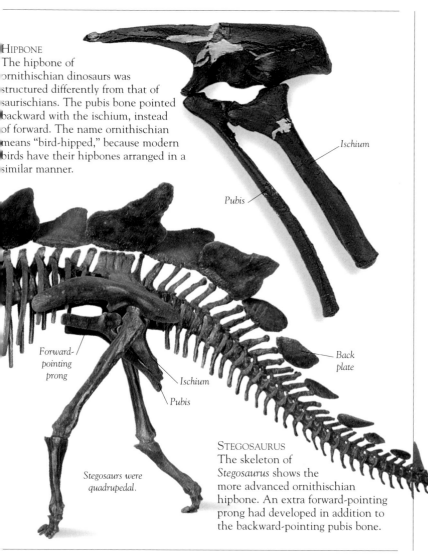

HIPBONE

The hipbone of ornithischian dinosaurs was structured differently from that of saurischians. The pubis bone pointed backward with the ischium, instead of forward. The name ornithischian means "bird-hipped," because modern birds have their hipbones arranged in a similar manner.

Ischium

Pubis

Forward-pointing prong

Ischium

Pubis

Back plate

Stegosaurs were quadrupedal.

STEGOSAURUS

The skeleton of *Stegosaurus* shows the more advanced ornithischian hipbone. An extra forward-pointing prong had developed in addition to the backward-pointing pubis bone.

STEGOSAURS

THE MOST NOTICEABLE features of the stegosaurs were the large plates, or spines, along an arched back. These plates may have regulated body temperature, and they may have also given protection, or even attracted a mate. Stegosaurs had small heads, and tiny brains no larger than a golf ball. The head was carried close to the ground for eating short, leafy plants and fruits.

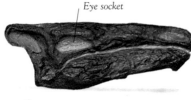

Eye socket

STEGOSAURUS SKULL
The skull of *Stegosaurus* was long and narrow. It had a toothless beak and small cheek teeth for chewing vegetation.

TAIL END
Stegosaurus is the most commonly known of all stegosaurs. It had long, horny spines on the end of its tail. With a quick swing of the tail, these spines could inflict a crippling stab to a predator, such as *Allosaurus*.

Spines had a sharp end.

PLATES AND SPINES
From above you can see the staggered plates along the top of *Stegosaurus'* body. This view also shows the tail spines pointing backward and outward – protection against attack from behind for when *Stegosaurus* was escaping.

Backward-pointing spines

Staggered plates

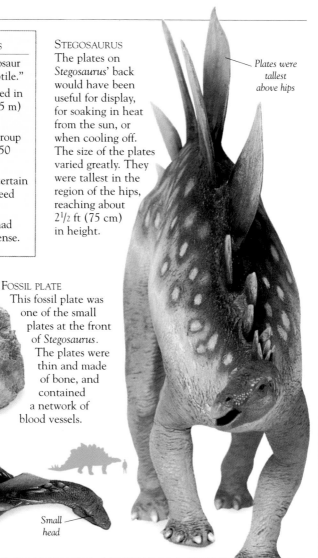

STEGOSAUR FACTS

- The name stegosaur means "plated reptile."

- Stegosaurs ranged in size from 15 ft (4.5 m) to 29½ ft (9 m).

- The stegosaur group survived for over 50 million years.

- They ate only certain plants, probably seed ferns and cycads.

- All stegosaurs had tail spines for defense.

STEGOSAURUS

The plates on *Stegosaurus*' back would have been useful for display, for soaking in heat from the sun, or when cooling off. The size of the plates varied greatly. They were tallest in the region of the hips, reaching about 2½ ft (75 cm) in height.

Plates were tallest above hips

FOSSIL PLATE

This fossil plate was one of the small plates at the front of *Stegosaurus*. The plates were thin and made of bone, and contained a network of blood vessels.

Small head

More stegosaurs

The front legs of stegosaurs were shorter than the rear legs. Stegosaurs may have reared up on their hind legs, balancing with their tail on the ground. The supple tail and powerful rear legs could have formed a tripod allowing stegosaurs to reach higher vegetation. The plates and spines may have been used for different purposes in different stegosaurs.

Cast of "second brain"

Cast of brain in skull

TWO BRAINS

It was once believed that stegosaurs had a second brain which filled a large cavity in the hips. But this is now known to have been a nerve center, which controlled the hind limbs and the tail.

TUOJIANGOSAURUS
Some scientists believe this reconstructed skeleton of *Tuojiangosaurus* to be wrong. They think the front limbs should be straighter, and not bent like a lizard's.

Large spines for wounding enemies

Tail was held off the ground

KENTROSAURUS
Six pairs of bony plates ran along the neck and shoulders of *Kentrosaurus*. Behind these plates were three pairs of flat spines and five pairs of long, sharp spines.

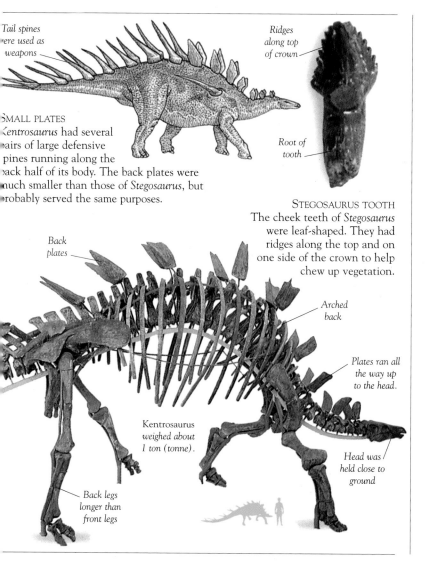

Tail spines were used as weapons

Ridges along top of crown

SMALL PLATES
Kentrosaurus had several pairs of large defensive spines running along the back half of its body. The back plates were much smaller than those of *Stegosaurus*, but probably served the same purposes.

Root of tooth

STEGOSAURUS TOOTH
The cheek teeth of *Stegosaurus* were leaf-shaped. They had ridges along the top and on one side of the crown to help chew up vegetation.

Back plates

Arched back

Plates ran all the way up to the head.

Kentrosaurus weighed about 1 ton (tonne).

Head was held close to ground

Back legs longer than front legs

ANKYLOSAURS

PROTECTED BY SPIKES and bony plates, the stocky ankylosaurs were the armored tanks of the dinosaur world. There were two main groups of ankylosaurs – the ankylosaurids and the nodosaurids.

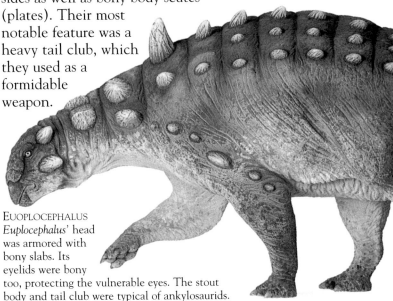

SKULL
The triangular skull of *Ankylosaurus* was covered with bony plates. It ended at a horny beak, which is used to crop vegetation.

Ankylosaurids

Many ankylosaurids had spines on their sides as well as bony body scutes (plates). Their most notable feature was a heavy tail club, which they used as a formidable weapon.

EUOPLOCEPHALUS
Euplocephalus' head was armored with bony slabs. Its eyelids were bony too, protecting the vulnerable eyes. The stout body and tail club were typical of ankylosaurids.

ANKYLOSAUR FACTS

- The name ankylosaur means "armored reptile."

- They ranged in length from 6 ft (1.8 m) to 29½ ft (9 m).

- They have been found on all continents, including Antarctica.

- All were covered in bony scutes on their upper side, but were unarmored on their lower side.

TAIL CLUB

The bony plates were good protection, but the tail club was an extremely effective weapon. A fearsome tyrannosaurid could be crippled with a well-directed blow to the ankle or shin.

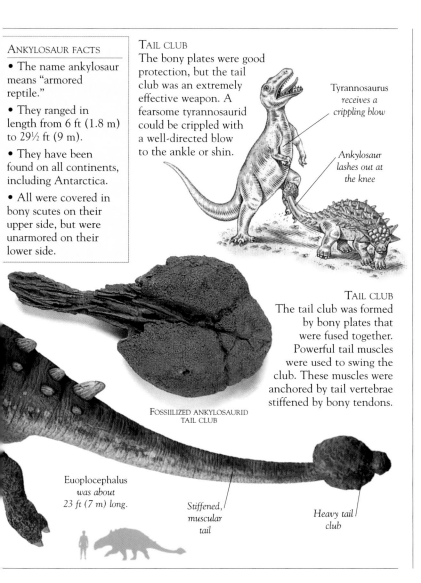

Tyrannosaurus *receives a crippling blow*

Ankylosaur *lashes out at the knee*

FOSSIILIZED ANKYLOSAURID TAIL CLUB

TAIL CLUB

The tail club was formed by bony plates that were fused together. Powerful tail muscles were used to swing the club. These muscles were anchored by tail vertebrae stiffened by bony tendons.

Euoplocephalus *was about 23 ft (7 m) long.*

Stiffened, muscular tail

Heavy tail club

101

Nodosaurids

Armored with bony plates and
dangerous spikes, but lacking the
clubbed tail of the ankylosaurids,
the nodosaurids were the most
primitive of the ankylosaurs. They
ranged in size from 5 ft (1.6 m)
to 25 ft (7.6 m) in length.
Nodosaurid fossils have
been found in rocks worldwide.

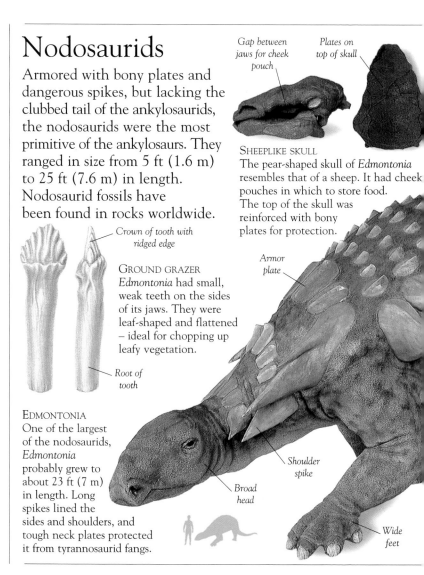

*Gap between
jaws for cheek
pouch*

*Plates on
top of skull*

SHEEPLIKE SKULL
The pear-shaped skull of *Edmontonia*
resembles that of a sheep. It had cheek
pouches in which to store food.
The top of the skull was
reinforced with bony
plates for protection.

*Crown of tooth with
ridged edge*

GROUND GRAZER
Edmontonia had small,
weak teeth on the sides
of its jaws. They were
leaf-shaped and flattened
– ideal for chopping up
leafy vegetation.

*Armor
plate*

*Root of
tooth*

EDMONTONIA
One of the largest
of the nodosaurids,
Edmontonia
probably grew to
about 23 ft (7 m)
in length. Long
spikes lined the
sides and shoulders, and
tough neck plates protected
it from tyrannosaurid fangs.

*Shoulder
spike*

*Broad
head*

*Wide
feet*

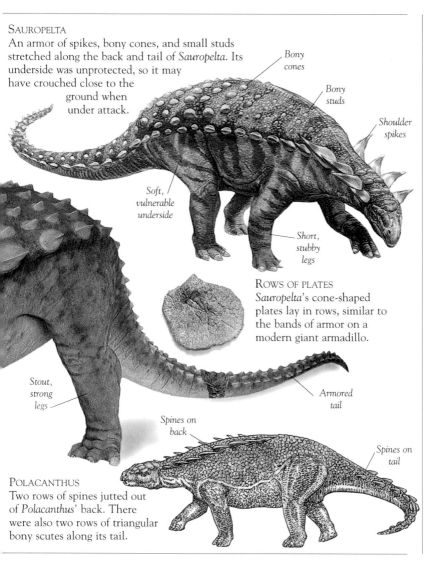

SAUROPELTA
An armor of spikes, bony cones, and small studs stretched along the back and tail of *Sauropelta*. Its underside was unprotected, so it may have crouched close to the ground when under attack.

Bony cones

Bony studs

Shoulder spikes

Soft, vulnerable underside

Short, stubby legs

ROWS OF PLATES
Sauropelta's cone-shaped plates lay in rows, similar to the bands of armor on a modern giant armadillo.

Stout, strong legs

Armored tail

Spines on back

Spines on tail

POLACANTHUS
Two rows of spines jutted out of *Polacanthus*' back. There were also two rows of triangular bony scutes along its tail.

ORNITHOPODS

ALL THE ORNITHOPOD dinosaurs were herbivores
with horned beaks. Their jaws and leaf-shaped
cheek teeth were ideal for chewing
vegetation. They were
bipedal, although some
of them may have foraged
for food on all fours.
Their feet had three or
four toes with hooflike
claws, and their hands
had four or five fingers.

Cheek teeth

Tusklike teeth

TOOTHY SKULL
Heterodontosaurus had three different
kinds of teeth. These were the front
upper teeth, which bit against the
toothless lower beak; the scissorlike
cheek teeth; and a pair of upper and
lower tusklike teeth.

GROUP LIVING
Hypsilophodon may have moved in herds
for protection against predatory theropods.
Moving as a large group, they would have
been able to warn each other of any danger,
giving them a better chance of survival.

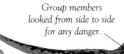

*Group members
looked from side to side
for any danger.*

*Slim, long
legs for speed*

Bony tendons

VERTEBRAE SUPPORT
Ornithopods such as *Iguanodon* had a crisscross of bony tendons strengthening the vertebrae above the hip and in the back. These bony tendons also stiffened the tail. This helped *Iguanodon* balance as it walked on its two back legs.

Toes ended in flattened hooves

ORNITHOPOD FACTS

• The name ornithopod means "bird foot."

• They ranged in length from 6½ ft (2 m) to 49 ft (15 m).

• Some ornithopods had up to 1,000 cheek teeth.

• They could run at speeds of at least 15 mph (9 km/h).

THREE-TOED FEET
The powerful three-toed feet of *Corythosaurus* were built to carry its heavy weight. *Corythosaurus* weighed approximately 4 tons (tonnes) and was about 24 ft (7.5 m) long. It belonged to a group of ornithopods called hadrosaurs.

Hypsilophodon was about 7½ ft (2.3 m) long.

Iguanodonts

These dinosaurs were bipedal herbivores with long toes that ended in hooflike claws. Their arms were thick and strong, and they may have often walked on all fours, perhaps when foraging for food. Iguanodonts had a single row of tall, ridged teeth, with which they chewed their food before swallowing it. The best-known iguanodonts are *Iguanodon* and *Ouranosaurus*.

Iguanodon stabbing a theropod in the neck

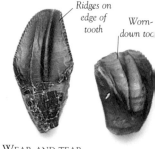

Ridges on edge of tooth

Worn-down too[th]

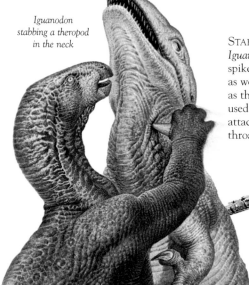

WEAR AND TEAR
The Iguanodon teeth above are a[t] different stages of wear. The one on the right has been worn down by Iguanodon's diet of tough plants, while the one on the left looks like it has hardly been used

STABBING WEAPON
Iguanodon had large, bony thumb spikes. These may have been used as weapons against enemies, such as theropods. *Iguanodon* may have used its thumb spike to stab an attacker through the throat, belly, or eyes.

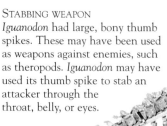

IGUANODON
The head of *Iguanodon* had a toothless beak for nipping vegetation. Its arms were much shorter than its hind legs, which ended in strong, three-toed feet to support its heavy weight. Its thick tail was very stiff, and was held out almost horizontally.

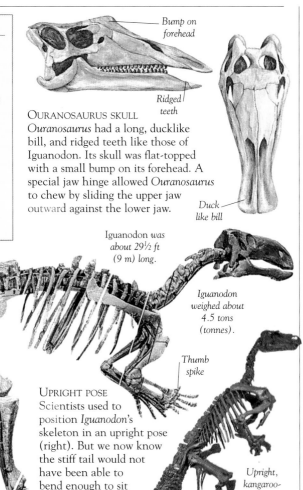

IGUANODONT FACTS

• The name iguanodont means "iguana tooth."

• They ranged in length from 13 ft (4 m) to 29½ ft (9 m).

• They lived from late Jurassic through to late Cretaceous periods.

• An *Iguanodon* shin bone found in 1809 was not identified as belonging to *Iguanodon* until the late 1970s.

Bump on forehead

Ridged teeth

OURANOSAURUS SKULL
Ouranosaurus had a long, ducklike bill, and ridged teeth like those of Iguanodon. Its skull was flat-topped with a small bump on its forehead. A special jaw hinge allowed *Ouranosaurus* to chew by sliding the upper jaw outward against the lower jaw.

Duck like bill

Iguanodon was about 29½ ft (9 m) long.

Iguanodon weighed about 4.5 tons (tonnes).

Thumb spike

Knee

Ankle

UPRIGHT POSE
Scientists used to position *Iguanodon*'s skeleton in an upright pose (right). But we now know the stiff tail would not have been able to bend enough to sit on the ground.

Upright, kangaroo-like pose is incorrect

107

Hadrosaurs

These herbivores are also known as "duckbills," because of their toothless, ducklike bills. Hundreds of self-sharpening teeth arranged in rows lined the sides of the jaws. Hadrosaurs were bipedal. They held their bodies horizontally with their stiffened tails extended for balance. There are two main groups of hadrosaurs: hadrosaurines, with flat-topped skulls, and lambeosaurines, with hollow head crests.

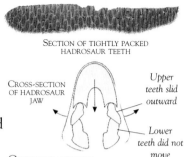

SECTION OF TIGHTLY PACKED HADROSAUR TEETH

CROSS-SECTION OF HADROSAUR JAW

Upper teeth slid outward

Lower teeth did not move

CHEWING ACTION
Hadrosaurs chewed food by grating the upper jaw teeth against the lower jaw teeth. The upper jaw was hinged so that when the jaws closed, the upper jaw would slide outward against the lower jaw.

Bony rods along spine

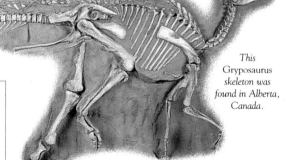

Deep tail

This Gryposaurus skeleton was found in Alberta, Canada.

HADROSAUR FACTS
• The name hadrosaur means "bulky lizard."
• They ranged in length from 10 ft (3 m) to 49 ft (15 m).
• They are known as the duck-billed dinosaurs because of their long, flat snouts.

GRYPOSAURUS
Like many hadrosaurs, *Gryposaurus* had a trellis of bony rods that stiffened the spine and tail. The deep tail would have been useful when swimming, and shows that hadrosaurs sometimes went into water. But they probably did this only when escaping from enemies.

CORYTHOSAURUS

Although *Corythosaurus* was bipedal, the hoof-shaped claws and padded toes on its hands indicate that it used them a lot for walking. Its diet included the toughest of plants, such as ferns and pine needles, but *Corythosaurus* could easily mash these using its rows of tightly packed teeth.

Hands could hold onto branches

Corythosaurus walked on all fours when feeding on ground-level plants.

Stiff tail was held out horizontally

109

Hadrosaurines

This group of hadrosaurs had little or no head crest, although some had a bump above the nose which they used for making noises. Some hadrosaurines had bills that curled upward, forming a spoon shape. They lived in North America, Europe, and Asia during the late Cretaceous period.

HADROSAUR FAMILY
Maiasaura bred in huge colonies, using the same nesting sites every year. The name Maiasaura means "good mother lizard"; *Maiasaura* cared for their young until they could fend for themselves.

Male Maiasaura feeding young

Eggs were laid in a mound made of earth and plant material

Female watches eggs

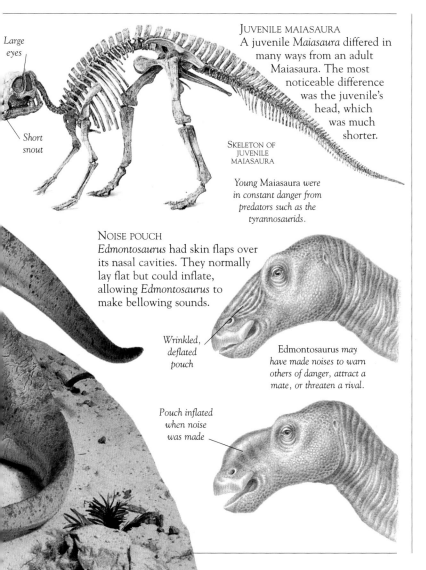

Large eyes

Short snout

JUVENILE MAIASAURA
A juvenile *Maiasaura* differed in many ways from an adult Maiasaura. The most noticeable difference was the juvenile's head, which was much shorter.

SKELETON OF JUVENILE MAIASAURA

Young Maiasaura were in constant danger from predators such as the tyrannosaurids.

NOISE POUCH
Edmontosaurus had skin flaps over its nasal cavities. They normally lay flat but could inflate, allowing *Edmontosaurus* to make bellowing sounds.

Wrinkled, deflated pouch

Edmontosaurus may have made noises to warn others of danger, attract a mate, or threaten a rival.

Pouch inflated when noise was made

Lambeosaurines

Large bony head crests were a dinstinctive feature of these hadrosaurs. Powerful limbs supported a heavy body, and the downward-curving lower jaw had a broad, blunt beak. They lived around the same time as the hadrosaurines, and their remains have been found in North America and Asia.

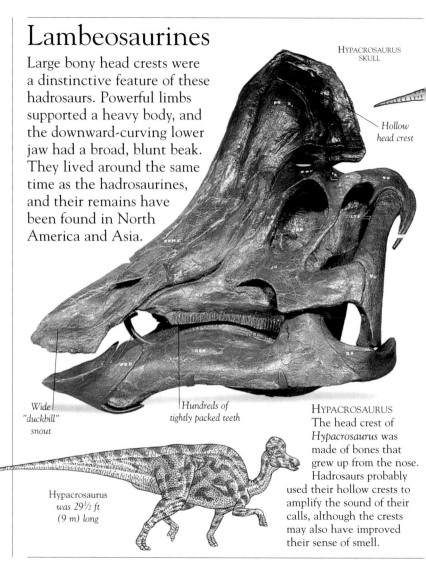

HYPACROSAURUS SKULL

Hollow head crest

Wide "duckbill" snout

Hundreds of tightly packed teeth

Hypacrosaurus was 29½ ft (9 m) long

HYPACROSAURUS
The head crest of *Hypacrosaurus* was made of bones that grew up from the nose. Hadrosaurs probably used their hollow crests to amplify the sound of their calls, although the crests may also have improved their sense of smell.

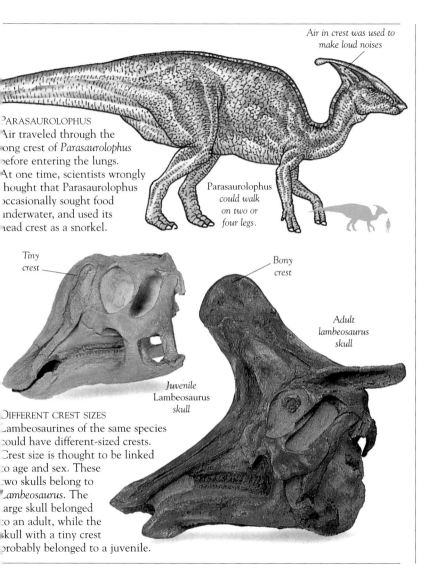

Air in crest was used to make loud noises

PARASAUROLOPHUS
Air traveled through the long crest of *Parasaurolophus* before entering the lungs. At one time, scientists wrongly thought that Parasaurolophus occasionally sought food underwater, and used its head crest as a snorkel.

Parasaurolophus could walk on two or four legs.

Tiny crest

Bony crest

Adult lambeosaurus skull

Juvenile Lambeosaurus *skull*

DIFFERENT CREST SIZES
Lambeosaurines of the same species could have different-sized crests. Crest size is thought to be linked to age and sex. These two skulls belong to *Lambeosaurus*. The large skull belonged to an adult, while the skull with a tiny crest probably belonged to a juvenile.

113

PACHYCEPHALOSAURS

THE THICK, DOMED skulls of pachycephalosaurs earned them the name "bone-headed dinosaurs." Rival males used to bash their heads together, their brains protected by the thick bone. Pachycephalosaurs probably had a good sense of smell, which would have allowed them to detect nearby predators and escape before the predators got too close.

HORN CLUSTER
Stygimoloch had a cluster of horns behind its dome. But the horns were probably just for show, rather than of practical use.

LOTS OF NODULES
Prenocephale's head had a well-developed solid dome and small nodules on the back of the skull.

PACHYCEPHALOSAUR FACTS

• The name pachycephalosaur means "thick-headed lizard."

• They ranged in length from 3 ft (90 cm) to 15 ft (4.6 m).

• Diet included fruits, leaves, and insects.

STEGOCERAS
Goat-sized *Stegoceras* was about 8 ft (2.4 m) long. Several *Stegoceras* skulls have been found with domes of various thicknesses. The domes of juveniles were not as thick or high as those of adults, especially adult males.

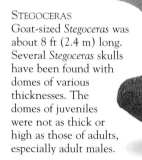

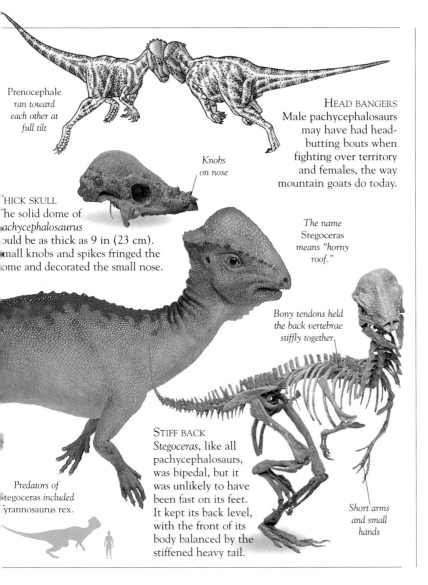

Prenocephale
*ran toward
each other at
full tilt*

*Knobs
on nose*

HEAD BANGERS
Male pachycephalosaurs
may have had head-
butting bouts when
fighting over territory
and females, the way
mountain goats do today.

THICK SKULL
The solid dome of
Pachycephalosaurus
could be as thick as 9 in (23 cm).
Small knobs and spikes fringed the
dome and decorated the small nose.

*The name
Stegoceras
means "horny
roof."*

*Bony tendons held
the back vertebrae
stiffly together*

STIFF BACK
Stegoceras, like all
pachycephalosaurs,
was bipedal, but it
was unlikely to have
been fast on its feet.
It kept its back level,
with the front of its
body balanced by the
stiffened heavy tail.

*Predators of
Stegoceras included
Tyrannosaurus rex.*

*Short arms
and small
hands*

CERATOPSIANS

HORNS, BONY FRILLS, and a parrotlike beak were the trademarks of the ceratopsians. They were all quadrupedal herbivores, and many ceratopsians lived in great herds. Most ceratopsians can be divided into two groups. One group had short neck frills, the other had long neck frills. The ceratopsians were among the last dinosaurs to become extinct.

PSITTACOSAURUS
SKULL

Psittacosaurus
*may have moved
on all fours
when foraging.*

PSITTACOSAURUS
This dinosaur was a 6½-ft-long
(2 m) bipedal ancestor of
the ceratopsians. It had
a parrotlike beak
and a very small
neck frill, but
lacked the horns
of ceratopsians.

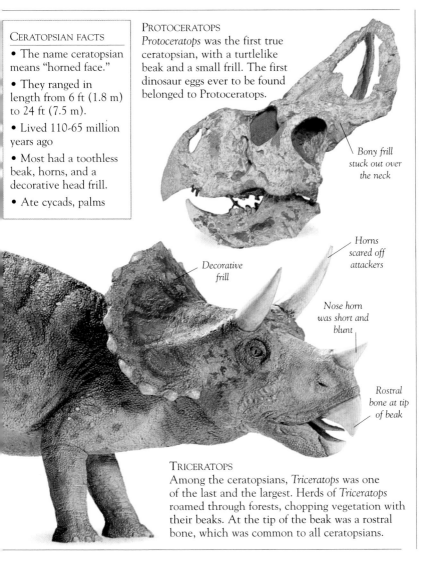

CERATOPSIAN FACTS

• The name ceratopsian means "horned face."

• They ranged in length from 6 ft (1.8 m) to 24 ft (7.5 m).

• Lived 110-65 million years ago

• Most had a toothless beak, horns, and a decorative head frill.

• Ate cycads, palms

PROTOCERATOPS
Protoceratops was the first true ceratopsian, with a turtlelike beak and a small frill. The first dinosaur eggs ever to be found belonged to Protoceratops.

Bony frill stuck out over the neck

Horns scared off attackers

Decorative frill

Nose horn was short and blunt

Rostral bone at tip of beak

TRICERATOPS
Among the ceratopsians, *Triceratops* was one of the last and the largest. Herds of *Triceratops* roamed through forests, chopping vegetation with their beaks. At the tip of the beak was a rostral bone, which was common to all ceratopsians.

Short-frilled ceratopsians

The group of ceratopsians with short frills also had long nose horns and short brow horns. *Styracosaurus* had the most dramatic frill, with long horns growing out from its edge. The discovery of five young near an adult *Brachyceratops* indicates that these ceratopsians looked after their young. It is likely that when a herd was in danger from predators, the males protected the young and the females.

STYRACOSAURUS SKULL

Long nose horn

STYRACOSAURUS
Six long spikes edged the frill of *Styracosaurus*. It had a lethal horn on its nose that was 2 ft (60 cm) long and 6 in (15 cm) thick. The horns above the eyes, however, were only stumps. It was possibly a good runner, capable of speeds of up to 20 mph (32 km/h).

Horns on edge of frill

Nose horn

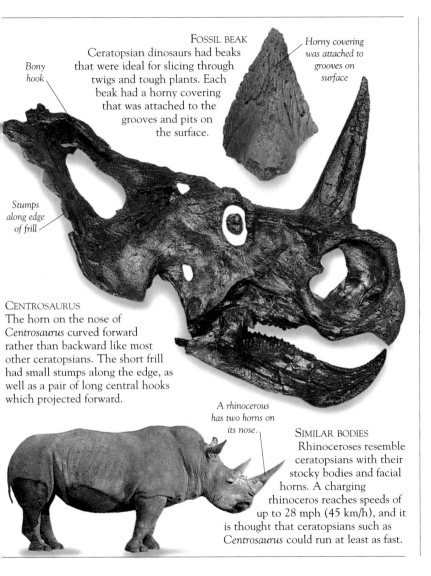

FOSSIL BEAK

Ceratopsian dinosaurs had beaks that were ideal for slicing through twigs and tough plants. Each beak had a horny covering that was attached to the grooves and pits on the surface.

Bony hook

Horny covering was attached to grooves on surface

Stumps along edge of frill

CENTROSAURUS

The horn on the nose of *Centrosaurus* curved forward rather than backward like most other ceratopsians. The short frill had small stumps along the edge, as well as a pair of long central hooks which projected forward.

A rhinocerous has two horns on its nose.

SIMILAR BODIES

Rhinoceroses resemble ceratopsians with their stocky bodies and facial horns. A charging rhinoceros reaches speeds of up to 28 mph (45 km/h), and it is thought that ceratopsians such as *Centrosaurus* could run at least as fast.

Long-frilled ceratopsians

The frill of long-frilled ceratopsians extended back to, or over, the shoulders. Sometimes the bony frill was armed with short spikes, and there were often holes in the frill to lighten the load. The snout had a short horn, and there were long brow horns – the opposite of the short-frilled ceratopsians.

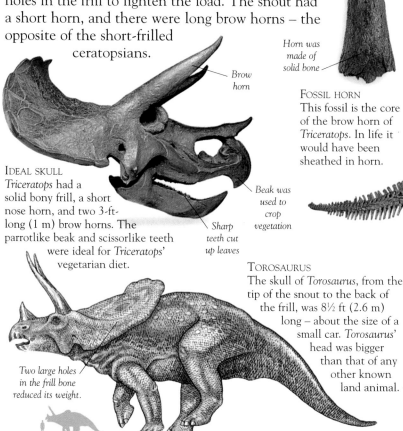

Brow horn

Horn was made of solid bone

FOSSIL HORN
This fossil is the core of the brow horn of *Triceratops*. In life it would have been sheathed in horn.

IDEAL SKULL
Triceratops had a solid bony frill, a short nose horn, and two 3-ft-long (1 m) brow horns. The parrotlike beak and scissorlike teeth were ideal for *Triceratops'* vegetarian diet.

Beak was used to crop vegetation

Sharp teeth cut up leaves

TOROSAURUS
The skull of *Torosaurus*, from the tip of the snout to the back of the frill, was 8½ ft (2.6 m) long – about the size of a small car. *Torosaurus'* head was bigger than that of any other known land animal.

Two large holes in the frill bone reduced its weight.

CHASMOSAURUS

The earliest long-frilled ceratopsian was *Chasmosaurus*. To lighten its weight, the frill had two large holes which were probably filled with muscle. Its skeleton was solidly built to bear its 2-ton (tonne) weight, and was not designed for speed. As with most ceratopsians, *Chasmosaurus* probably had few predators and used its horns mostly in territorial disputes.

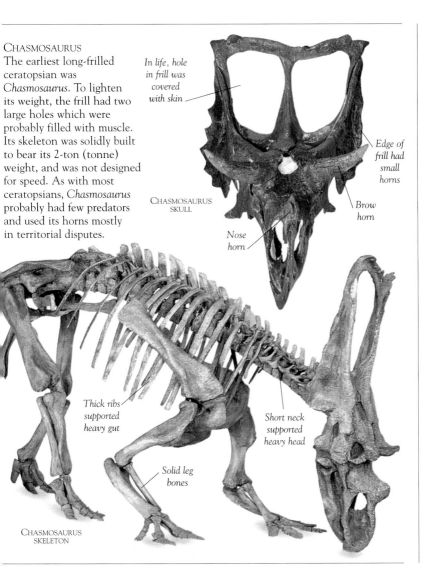

In life, hole in frill was covered with skin

Edge of frill had small horns

CHASMOSAURUS SKULL

Brow horn

Nose horn

Thick ribs supported heavy gut

Short neck supported heavy head

Solid leg bones

CHASMOSAURUS SKELETON

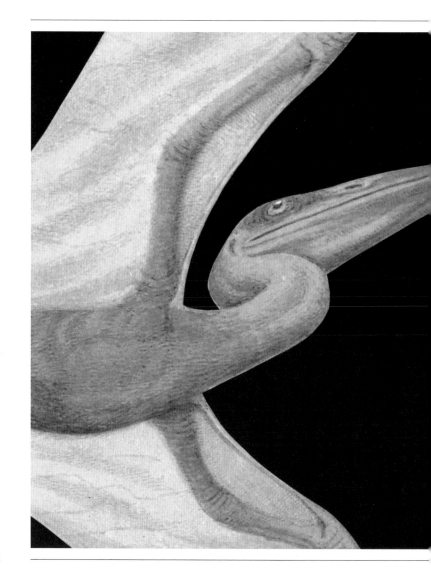

REPTILES OF THE SEA AND AIR

ABOUT SEA AND AIR REPTILES

WHILE THE DINOSAURS lived on land, other reptiles lived in the sea and flew in the air. The sea reptiles, such as the ichthyosaurs and plesiosaurs, needed to breathe air and would have surfaced frequently to fill their lungs. The flying reptiles, called pterosaurs, included the largest ever flying animals. There were two groups of pterosaur – rhamphorhynchoids and pterodactyloids.

Wing made of skin

Clawed foot

Furry body

Sharp teeth in long beak

Short tail

Clawed fingers

Pterodactylus was a small pterosaur with a wingspan of only 20 in (50 cm).

FUR FOR WARMTH
Pterodactylus was a pterodactyloid from the Jurassic period. Some *Pterodactylus* fossils showed small furlike impressions around the body. This suggests that pterosaurs may have been warm blooded and would have used fur to keep themselves warm.

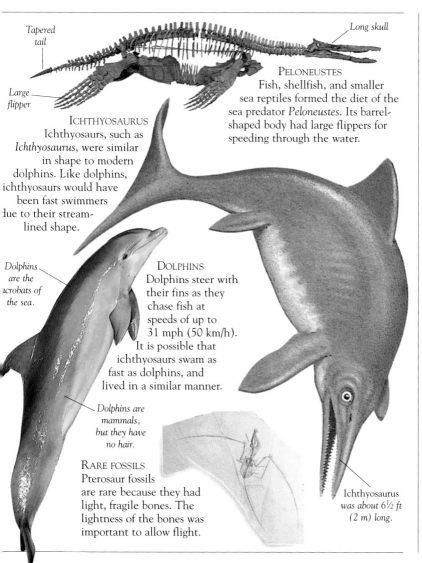

Tapered tail

Long skull

Large flipper

PELONEUSTES
Fish, shellfish, and smaller sea reptiles formed the diet of the sea predator *Peloneustes*. Its barrel-shaped body had large flippers for speeding through the water.

ICHTHYOSAURUS
Ichthyosaurs, such as *Ichthyosaurus*, were similar in shape to modern dolphins. Like dolphins, ichthyosaurs would have been fast swimmers due to their stream-lined shape.

Dolphins are the acrobats of the sea.

DOLPHINS
Dolphins steer with their fins as they chase fish at speeds of up to 31 mph (50 km/h). It is possible that ichthyosaurs swam as fast as dolphins, and lived in a similar manner.

Dolphins are mammals, but they have no hair.

RARE FOSSILS
Pterosaur fossils are rare because they had light, fragile bones. The lightness of the bones was important to allow flight.

Ichthyosaurus was about 6½ ft (2 m) long.

REPTILES AT SEA

THE SEA REPTILES evolved from land reptiles that adapted to life in the water. The legs and feet shortened and widened to become paddles, and the body became streamlined for faster movement through water. These reptiles were carnivores, preying on other sea creatures as well as each other.

MODIFIED PADDLE
The plesiosaur *Cryptoclidus* was 13 ft (4 m) long and had four paddles that were each about 3 ft (1 m) long. It swam by flexing these powerful paddles up and down, "flying" through the water in the way that penguins do today.

Each paddle had five elongated toes.

Large and sharp teeth

Curved and conical teeth

Powerful, flexible paddles propelled Pliosaurus through the water.

FLEXIBLE JAWS
Masosaurus was a giant marine lizard which lived in late Cretaceous shallow coastal waters. The skull and lower jaw bones had flexible joints and curved, piercing teeth. This would enable *Masosaurus* to give a wide and lethal bite.

All plesiosaurs had very long necks and small heads.

PHOTOGRAPH TAKEN
AT LOCH NESS

Could this be the Loch Ness Monster?

MYSTERIOUS MONSTER

Many people claim to have seen a large creature swimming in Loch Ness in Scotland. This animal, known as the Loch Ness Monster, has been described as a living relative of the plesiosaurs.

MURAENOSAURUS

Air-filled lungs meant that the plesiosaur *Muraenosaurus* would have found it easier to float than to dive underwater. To combat this, it probably swallowed pebbles to weigh itself down, the way that crocodiles do today.

Scaly skin

Tail flipper

The skin would have been scaly, like the reptiles on land.

PLIOSAURUS

One of the fiercest predators of its time, *Pliosaurus* hunted in the seas of the Jurassic period 150 million years ago. It was about 23 ft (7 m) long and fed on fish and smaller sea reptiles. Like all pliosaurs, *Pliosaurus* had a short neck, a large head, and a barrel-shaped body. It also had strong jaws and large, sharp teeth with which it could crush and kill prey.

SEA REPTILE FACTS

- They breathed air.
- They were carnivores.
- The turtles are the only sea reptiles still living.
- Ichthyosaurs bore live young; all other reptiles laid eggs.

More reptiles at sea

Plesiosaurs, pliosaurs, and turtles probably hauled themselves onto beaches to lay eggs, the way modern turtles do. Ichthyosaurs did not leave the water since they were fully adapted to life at sea and gave birth to live young. By the time the dinosaurs died out, all sea reptiles, apart from the turtles, had become extinct, too. The reason for this is as mysterious as the disappearance of the dinosaurs.

Fossil shell of th[...] 12-in-long (30 cm) turtle Cimochelys

FOSSIL SHELLS
Fossilized ancient turtle shells show that these turtles had the same bony armor as modern turtles.

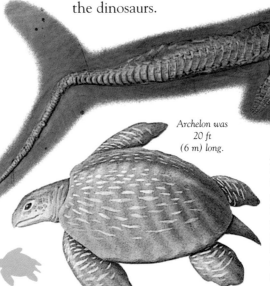

Archelon was 20 ft (6 m) long.

ARCHELON
Like its descendants, the modern turtles, *Archelon* may have returned to the same beaches every year to lay eggs. Both the adult *Archelon* and its eggs would have been vulnerable to predatory dinosaurs of that time.

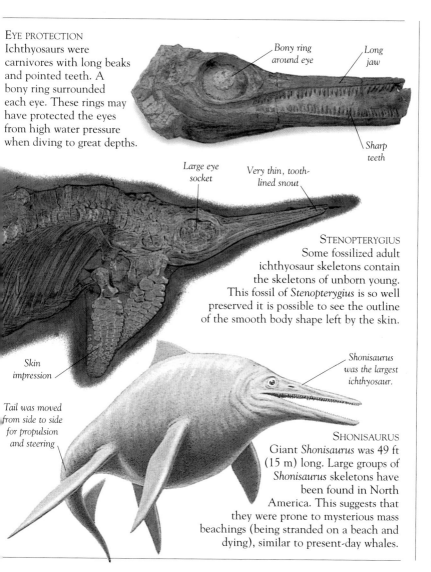

EYE PROTECTION
Ichthyosaurs were
carnivores with long beaks
and pointed teeth. A
bony ring surrounded
each eye. These rings may
have protected the eyes
from high water pressure
when diving to great depths.

Bony ring
around eye

Long
jaw

Sharp
teeth

Large eye
socket

Very thin, tooth-
lined snout

STENOPTERYGIUS
Some fossilized adult
ichthyosaur skeletons contain
the skeletons of unborn young.
This fossil of *Stenopterygius* is so well
preserved it is possible to see the outline
of the smooth body shape left by the skin.

Skin
impression

Shonisaurus
was the largest
ichthyosaur.

Tail was moved
from side to side
for propulsion
and steering

SHONISAURUS
Giant *Shonisaurus* was 49 ft
(15 m) long. Large groups of
Shonisaurus skeletons have
been found in North
America. This suggests that
they were prone to mysterious mass
beachings (being stranded on a beach and
dying), similar to present-day whales.

REPTILES IN THE AIR

THE PTEROSAURS were the first ever flying vertebrates (animals with a backbone). Their wings were a thin membrane of muscles and elastic fibers covered with skin. The rhamphorhynchoid group of pterosaurs had long tails and short heads with sharp teeth. They first appeared in the Triassic period and became extinct at the end of the Jurassic period.

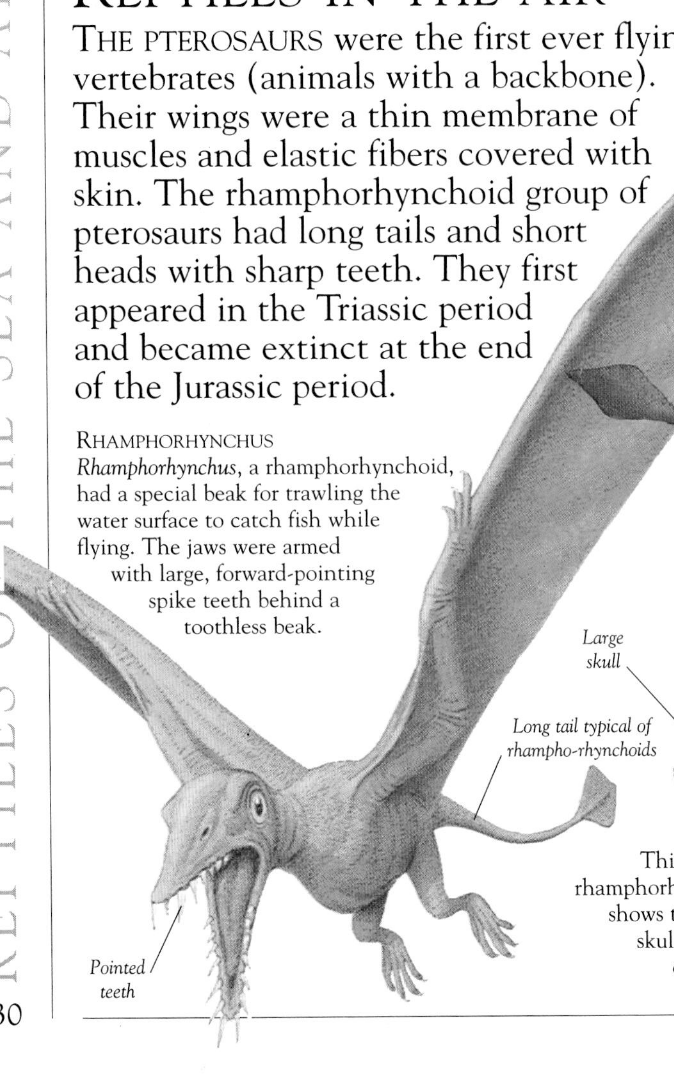

RHAMPHORHYNCHUS
Rhamphorhynchus, a rhamphorhynchoid, had a special beak for trawling the water surface to catch fish while flying. The jaws were armed with large, forward-pointing spike teeth behind a toothless beak.

Stiff tail may have been used for steering when flying

Large skull

Long tail typical of rhampho-rhynchoids

Pointed teeth

FOSSIL
This fossil skeleton of the rhamphorhynchoid *Dimorphodon* shows the fine bones and the skull which was very large compared to the body

SORDES
A thick coat
of insulating "hair"
covered *Sordes'* body. But
its hairs were not like the
hairs of a mammal – they
probably developed from reptile
scales, like the feathers of a bird.

AIR REPTILE FACTS
• The pterosaurs
included the largest
ever flying animals.

• Their wings were
made of muscles,
elastic fibers, and skin.

• They were
carnivores, eating fish,
insects, and small
reptiles.

• The last of the
pterosaurs died out
with the dinosaurs.

*Elongated
fourth finger
supporting
wing*

*Clawed
fingers*

*Large, deep
snout with
sharp teeth*

*Dimorphodon lived
190 million years ago
and was one of the first
pterosaurs.*

*Wing
covered
with skin*

*Dimorphodon
had a wingspan of
4½ ft (1.4 m).*

*The legs were powerful,
which suggests that they
were used for walking
and running.*

DIMORPHODON
Like all pterosaurs, the
wings of *Dimorphodon*
were supported by
an elongated fourth
finger. The other
three fingers on *Dimorphodon's* hands
were large and clawed and may
have been used for climbing
rocks and cliffs.

131

More reptiles in the air

The pterodactyloid group of pterosaurs included the largest animals ever to take to the air. Pterodactyloids had long heads, long necks, and short tails. The head had a large crest, which may have acted as a counterbalance to the long beak. Some pterodactyloids had specialized teeth, such as *Pterodaustro*, whose teeth were bristlelike for filtering food. Most pterodactyloids would have skimmed the water surface for fish with their long jaws.

PTERANODON
The head of *Pteranodon* was 6 ft (1.8 m) long from the tip of its beak to the back of its crest. Some *Pteranodon* fossils lack a crest, which may have been a difference between the sexes.

Head crest

Pointed beak

Long, curved neck

Short tail

Clawed feet

Toothless beak

WING FINGER
This is a fossilized bone from Pteranodon's elongated wing finger. The wing finger consisted of long, thin, and very light bones which extended to the tip of the wing. Pteranodon was one of the largest pterosaurs, with a wingspan of 23 ft (7 m).

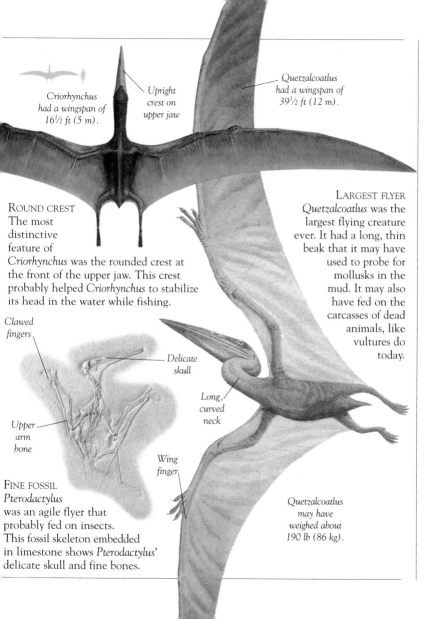

Criorhynchus had a wingspan of 16½ ft (5 m).

Upright crest on upper jaw

Quetzalcoatlus had a wingspan of 39½ ft (12 m).

ROUND CREST
The most distinctive feature of *Criorhynchus* was the rounded crest at the front of the upper jaw. This crest probably helped *Criorhynchus* to stabilize its head in the water while fishing.

Clawed fingers

Delicate skull

Upper arm bone

Wing finger

FINE FOSSIL
Pterodactylus was an agile flyer that probably fed on insects. This fossil skeleton embedded in limestone shows *Pterodactylus'* delicate skull and fine bones.

LARGEST FLYER
Quetzalcoatlus was the largest flying creature ever. It had a long, thin beak that it may have used to probe for mollusks in the mud. It may also have fed on the carcasses of dead animals, like vultures do today.

Long, curved neck

Quetzalcoatlus may have weighed about 190 lb (86 kg).

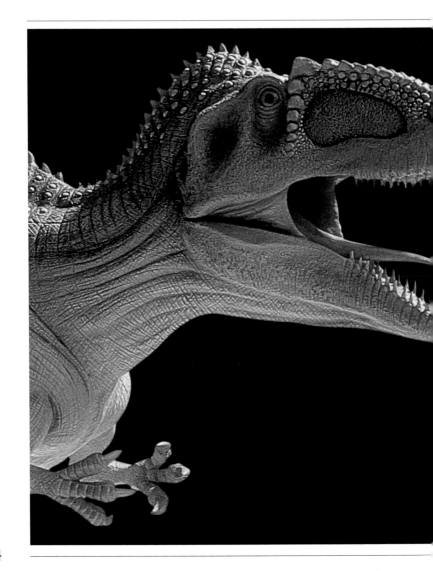

DINOSAUR FACTS

DINOSAUR PIONEERS

The first people known to discover, study, and identify dinosaur remains:

- British canal engineer William Smith uncovered some giant bones in Sussex between 1807 and 1809. They were later identified as those of an *Iguanodon*.

- Dr. Gideon Mantell and his wife Mary found the remains of *Iguanodon* in Sussex, England, in 1822, but did not name them until 1825.

- The name "Dinosauria" was invented by British anatomist Sir Richard Owen in 1841 to describe these newly discovered animals.

- The first American dinosaur bones were described and named by Joseph Leidy in 1858. These were from the "duckbill" *Hadrosaurus*.

THE "SEA DRAGONS"

Fossils of sea animals are much more common than fossils of land animals such as dinosaurs. In the early part of the 19th century such creatures were referred to as "sea dragons."

- The best known fossil hunter of the early 19th century was Mary Anning (1799-1847). With her brother Joseph, she found many ichthyosaur skeletons along the coast of Dorset, England.

- Mary and her brother were the first to find a complete plesiosaur skeleton in 1823.

- Most of the early finds of fossil marine animals disappeared into private collections, although the British Museum managed to acquire a small number.

- This early activity in the study of marine reptile fossils laid the foundations for the dinosaur research of later years.

Remains of ichthyosaurs were among the earliest finds of prehistoric creatures.

THE BERNISSART IGUANODONS

The story of the first complete dinosaur skeletons to be found:

- In 1887, miners in in Bernissart, Belgium, found a deposit of bones representing the remains of 39 *Iguanodons*. Most of them were complete and articulated.

- This discovery confirmed that some dinosaurs stood on their hind legs – an idea put forward by Joseph Leidy after studying the bones of *Hadrosaurus*.

- French-born mining engineer Louis Dollo devoted 40 years of his life to studying the Bernissart *Iguanodons* for the Brussels Museum.

- In the 1930s, the bones were covered in a protective material. When it was cleaned off in the 1980s, new studies revealed important details about the teeth.

Iguanodon – one of the first dinosaurs to be identified.

THE "BONE WARS"

The "Bone Wars" was a period of intense rivalry between two American paleontologists, Edward Drinker Cope and Othniel Charles Marsh.

- The rivalry began in 1870, when Cope mounted a skeleton of a plesiosaur with the skull on the wrong end. Marsh pointed out the error and Cope never forgave him.

- Both men hired teams to search for dinosaur remains in Colorado and Wyoming. Fights broke out between them and each team destroyed remains to stop them from being found by their rivals.

- Sometimes, Cope named an animal and Marsh gave it a completely different name – a mess that had to be cleared up later.

- The result of all this rivalry was the discovery of nearly 140 new kinds of dinosaur by the beginning of the 20th century.

DINOSAUR FACTS

THE GERMAN EXPEDITIONS TO AFRICA

- In 1907, dinosaur remains were found in Africa, near Tendaguru in what is now Tanzania. An expedition from the Berlin Museum of Natural History was sent there in 1909-1912.

- 500 local workers were used in the excavations and 1,000 boxes of fossils were shipped to Germany.

- The most spectacular skeleton was that of *Brachiosaurus*, which was subsequently mounted in the Humboldt Museum. For many decades it was the biggest mounted dinosaur skeleton in existence.

- Later expeditions, led by Ernst Stromer between 1910 and 1914, found dinosaur remains in El-Bahariya in Egypt.

- The El-Bahariya site was lost until 1999, when an American team using Stromer's notes identified a hill from its description. Valuable dinosaur remains have since been found there.

THE AMERICAN EXPEDITIONS TO MONGOLIA

- In 1921, an expedition from the American Museum of Natural History, led by Roy Chapman Andrews, entered Mongolia looking for human remains. Instead they found dinosaur fossils.

- The open desert landscape proved to be excellent for fossil-finding. The first dinosaur eggs to be identified as such were found on this expedition.

- At the time, the eggs were thought to have been laid by the horned dinosaur *Protoceratops*. They are now known to have come from the *Oviraptor* – a dinosaur that may have been an egg stealer.

- It was the most important land-based scientific expedition in American history.

Oviraptor – *"egg thief"*

AMATEUR DISCOVERIES

- Amateur fossil hunter William Walker found *Baryonyx* in 1983, while he was digging for fossils in a clay pit in southern England.

- Modern excavations have to rely on volunteer help. There is little financing to pay for a professional workforce.

- The longest dinosaur known, *Seismosaurus*, was found by Arthur Loy and Jan Cummings in New Mexico in 1979. They had been looking for native American rock paintings.

William Walker, pictured holding a Baryonyx claw.

- *Giganotosaurus* was discovered in Argentina by car mechanic Ruben Carolini. This huge dinosaur has been given the scientific name *Giganotosaurus carolinii* in his honor.

TECHNIQUES AND TECHNOLOGY

- Modern paleontologists pay as much attention to the rocks in which the fossils are found as they do to the fossils themselves. This allows a picture of the contemporary environment to be built up.

- Dinosaur bones are fragile. They are encased in plaster or polyurethane foam to protect them as they are moved from the site. Helicopters can now be used to transport heavy fossils from remote areas.

- Some fossil bones are slightly radioactive. In such instances, it has been possible to locate the bones using a Geiger counter.

- The use of radar can sometimes accurately locate dinosaur remains without the need for digging. This can save valuable time and money on an expedition.

DINOSAUR FACTS

THE TRIASSIC WORLD

- The Triassic period began 245 million years ago and lasted 37 million years. The dinosaurs evolved toward the end of this period.

- Before this time, the main land-dwelling animals were the mammal like reptiles. They died out and the dinosaurs took over. Mammals appeared at the same time as the dinosaurs.

- In the Triassic period, all the landmasses of the world were joined together as one large continent, known as Pangaea. A single ocean named Panthalassa covered the rest of the world.

- Only the coastal areas of Pangaea would have been habitable, as the climate of the interior was extremely hot and dry. The main plant life at the time consisted of conifers, cycads, ferns, and horsetails.

- The end of the period was marked by a mass extinction. 90% of large animals died out, but smaller animals fared better.

THE JURASSIC WORLD

- The Jurassic period began 208 million years ago and lasted 62 million years. It is often known as the "age of reptiles" because the dinosaurs were the dominant creatures on land.

- Pangaea began to break up during this period. Rift valleys split up the land into sections that would eventually form the modern continents. Herds of dinosaurs migrated from one area to another.

- The climate became wetter and less extreme as the seasons developed. Shallow seas spread across the continent and new oceans began to grow along the rifts.

- There were still widespread areas of dry desert and the main plant types were similar to those of the Triassic.

Skeleton of Sinokannemeyeria – *a mammal-like reptile of the early Triassic.*

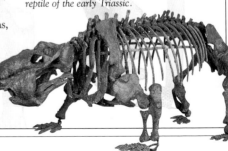

THE CRETACEOUS WORLD

- The Cretaceous period began 145 million years ago and lasted for 81 million years.

- Most of the continents had divided roughly into their modern shapes and were drifting apart. There were still no polar ice caps.

- Plant life began to change, with modern types of seed-bearing plants appearing.

- Plant-eating dinosaurs began to eat a wider range of vegetation. This could account for the spurt in plant evolution.

- In the latter half of the period there were widespread shallow seas across the continents, in which chalk was deposited.

- The end of the period saw one of the biggest mass extinctions in the Earth's history – all of the dinosaurs were wiped out.

THE WORLD AFTER THE DINOSAURS

- Only 65 million years have passed since the dinosaurs died, compared with the 150 million years in which they thrived.

- With the dinosaurs and other big reptiles extinct, the mammals became the dominant creatures on land. Birds began to thrive.

- At first, many kinds of unusual mammals evolved, as if nature were experimenting with evolution.

- Grass began to grow and large areas of grassland spread over the continents. This led to the evolution of grazing mammals.

- Human beings did not appear until sometime during the last age, around 35,000-100,000 years ago.

An artist's impression of a Cretaceous scene.

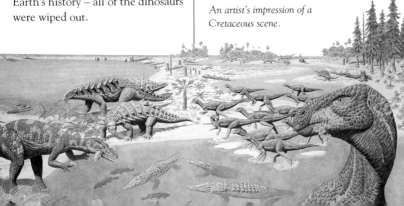

141

THE FIRST DINOSAURS

- Dinosaurs belong to a group of animals called the archosaurs. The pterosaurs (flying reptiles) and crocodiles are part of the same group.

- Before the dinosaurs, the most important land animals were the mammal-like reptiles. These died out as the dinosaurs appeared.

- Most of the archosaurs of the Triassic period were semiaquatic crocodile-like creatures. Dinosaurs probably evolved from these.

- The earliest dinosaurs are thought to be small meat eaters from Triassic South America – *Staurikosaurus*, *Eoraptor*, and *Herrerasaurus*.

- Many scientists believe that dinosaurs evolved in South America and spread throughout Pangaea.

SMALL THEROPODS

- All the meat-eating dinosaurs belong to the group called the theropods.

- As a rule, meat-eating animals are smaller bodied than plant-eating animals. This is because eating meat requires a far smaller digestive system.

- Very small meat eaters, such as *Compsognathus*, ate lizards and insects. Slightly larger creatures, such as *Velociraptor*, probably hunted in packs, preying on much bigger animals.

Compsognathus – *one of the smallest dinosaurs – was about the size of a chicken.*

- Most meat eaters had straight, stiff tails that they used for balance. This allowed some of them to run very fast, up to 25 mph (40 km/h).

- Many experts believe that birds evolved from the small meat eaters.

DINOSAUR FACTS

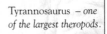

BIG THEROPODS

- For a century, *Tyrannosaurus* was regarded as the biggest meat-eating dinosaur.

- In the 1990s, the skeletons of two meat eaters came to light, *Giganotosaurus* and *Carcharodontosaurus*, each longer than *Tyrannosaurus*.

- Paleontologists still argue over whether the big meat-eating dinosaurs were active hunters or slow-moving scavengers.

- Some experts point to the fact that theropods had short thighbones in relation to the rest of the leg. This suggests that the legs were designed for running at high speed.

Tyrannosaurus – one of the largest theropods.

- Others point out that the theropods had hollow limb bones. While this made them relatively light, the suggestion is that the weaker, hollow bones made them susceptible to serious injury, particularly if they fell over at speed.

SEGNOSAURS

- The segnosaurs have puzzled many experts, being meat-eating dinosaurs but with some features very much like plant eaters.

- Their remains have been found in rocks from the late Cretaceous period.

- Segnosaur fossils were first found in 1933, when they were thought to be parts of a *Tyrannosaurus*. It was not until the late 1970s that they were recognized as a distinct dinosaur group.

- They had small heads with fine teeth, leading some paleontologists to think that they were fish eaters. However, a beak at the front of the mouth suggests a diet that consisted mainly of plants.

- Very long claws on the hands have led to speculation that they fed like anteaters, tearing into termite mounds and eating the contents.

- Recent discoveries in China show that some segnosaurs were covered in feathers, suggesting that they could be close relatives of birds.

PLANT EATERS

PROSAUROPODS

- The prosauropods were the first big plant-eating dinosaurs. They lived in the late Triassic and early Jurassic periods.

- They were once thought to have been the ancestors of the sauropods, having features of both the early ancestral meat eaters and the later long-necked plant eaters.

- Their long necks would have allowed them to reach leaves at the tops of high trees.

- They probably walked mainly on all fours and reared up on their hind legs to reach even higher. Their considerable weight was concentrated around the hips.

- Some were small and rabbit-sized, while the biggest was 26-33 ft (8-10 meters) long.

SAUROPODS

- The sauropods were the long-necked plant eaters. They were the biggest land animals that ever walked the Earth.

- Most sauropods walked on all fours. Their large digestive system was carried forward of the lizard-shaped hips and made it difficult to balance on hind legs.

- Some sauropods, like *Diplodocus*, were long and low and able to rise up on to their hind legs for short periods to browse on leaves. Others, such as the 39 ft- (12 meter-) high *Brachiosaurus*, simply relied on their enormous height.

- One group of sauropods, the titanosaurs, flourished at the end of the Cretaceous. They had armored backs, but the armor was probably used for stiffening the backbone rather than for defense.

Diplodocus was one of the longest sauropods, measuring up to 86 ft (26 meters).

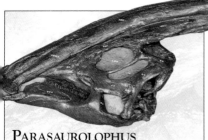

PARASAUROLOPHUS

This skull of *Parasaurolophus*, a duckbill, shows its unusual head crest. It is thought that the dinosaur used the hollow, tubelike structure to create a distinctive bellowing sound.

SMALL ORNITHOPODS

- Ornithopods were the two-footed plant eaters. They lived throughout the dinosaur era – from the late Triassic to the end of the Cretaceous.

- They had a beak at the front of the mouth and cheeks on the side.

- Birdlike hips allowed their big, plant-eating intestines to be carried toward the back, allowing the animal to balance for a two-footed way of life.

- Small ornithopods were fast-running animals – none of them had heavy horns or armor.

- They usually had four or five fingers, rather than the two or three found on the theropods.

BIG ORNITHOPODS

- The bigger ornithopods, such as *Iguanodon*, probably spent most of their time down on all fours. When young, they may have run about on hind legs, just like the smaller ornithopods.

- Their well-developed jaws and teeth could grind up food very well. Their hands and feet had hooves and weight-bearing pads.

- One group – the "duckbills" – were the most important plant eaters at the end of the Cretaceous period.

- There were two groups of duckbills. The hadrosaurines had flat heads; the lambeosaurines had flamboyant head crests. Both groups had toothless beaks.

- It is thought that the duckbills had a well-developed system of communicating by sound. The lambeosaurines used their crests, while the hadrosaurines used the inflatable flaps above their beaks.

- They lived in herds, finding safety in sheer numbers.

DINOSAUR FACTS

CERATOPSIANS

- The ceratopsians were the horned dinosaurs. Sometimes they are called the "ceratopians" – without the middle "s." They existed at the end of the Cretaceous period.

- The earliest were the pstittacosaurs – the "parrot reptiles." They were similar to ornithopods, but with big, parrotlike heads.

- The later types can be divided into two groups. The centrosaurines had long horns on the nose and short neck shields; the chasmosaurines had long horns above the eyes and long neck shields.

- The horns and shields may have been used primarily for display, rather than for fighting.

- Bone beds consisting of the fossils of hundreds of individuals suggest that ceratopsians migrated in herds.

PACHYCEPHALOSAURS

- Pachycephalosaurs – the "boneheads" – were closely related to the ceratopsians. Like that group, they lived at the end of the Cretaceous period.

- They all had a bony helmet over the skull, believed to have been used like a battering ram.

- Dinosaur skulls are usually very rare. Pachycephalosaur skulls are very solid and have fossilized well. A relatively large number have been found.

- *Pachycephalosaurus* was up to 26 ft (8 m) long and was the largest of this group. Most pachycephalosaurs were very small dinosaurs.

- The earliest example was found in early Cretaceous rocks on the Isle of Wight, England. Others have been discovered in late Cretaceous rock in Asia and North America.

THREE HORNS

Triceratops – "three-horned face" – was the biggest of the ceratopsians and had the most striking horns and neck frill. It is easy to imagine these rhinoceros-like creatures locking horns with one another in combat.

STEGOSAURS

- The stegosaurs were the "plated" dinosaurs. They all had plates and spines in different arrangements down their backs.

- Stegosaurs evolved in the early Jurassic period. They became very common in the late Jurassic and early Cretaceous and then they died away.

- Most stegosaurs had a heavily spiked tail – sometimes called a "thagomizer" – that they used to defend themselves.

- It is thought that those with the broadest plates, such as *Stegosaurus*, used them to collect heat from the Sun and to funnel cool breezes across their bodies, rather than for defense.

Stegosaurus was the largest of all the known stegosaurs.

ANKYLOSAURS

- The ankylosaurs were heavily armored dinosaurs. The armor consisted of a mosaic of flat, bony plates that stretched from the head to the end of the tail. Some even had armor on their eyelids.

- There are two types, the ankylosaurids, which had a bony club at the end of the tail, and the nodosaurids, which had rows of spikes along the sides of the body. Both lived in the late Cretaceous period.

- The ankylosaurids had broad jaws and took wide mouthfuls of vegetation. The nodosaurids had narrow jaws and were more selective about their food.

- Most ankylosaur fossils are of armor lying upside down. It is thought that they were washed down rivers with the weight of their armor turning them over as they went.

PANGAEAN DINOSAURS

- Similar animals lived in different parts of Pangaea – the Earth's original, single landmass.

- The small theropod *Coelophysis*, from New Mexico, was almost identical to the small theropod *Syntarsus* from Zimbabwe, Africa.

- The prosauropods of South Africa were almost the same as those of central Europe.

- Pterosaurs – the flying reptiles – developed in Pangaea at the same as the dinosaurs.

Coelophysis, one of the earliest dinosaurs, would have been found in Pangaea.

NORTHERN HEMISPHERE DINOSAURS

- Pangaea was a single landmass, but it was divided into Laurasia to the north and Gondwana to the south by an inlet of ocean, called the Tethys – an area around what is now central and southern Europe.

- Remains of dwarf dinosaurs (duckbills and ankylosaurs the size of sheep) have been found in what were Cretaceous islands in the Tethys. They probably adapted to the limited resources of island habitats.

- In the late Jurassic and Cretaceous periods, a shallow seaway stretched north-south across North America. Dinosaur footprints point north and south too, as if the animals were following the coastline.

- During the Cretaceous summers, plant eaters probably migrated into the polar areas of the far north to take advantage of the short growing season.

- Cretaceous northern Asia and North America were a single landmass. The same types of dinosaurs lived in both places.

SOUTHERN HEMISPHERE DINOSAURS

- The dinosaurs of Gondwana became significantly different from those of Laurasia in the early Cretaceous period.

- Excavations in Madagascar, which began in 1995, showed that the dinosaurs of that island were more similar to those of South America than to those of nearby Africa.

- There was probably a land bridge between South America and Africa until the early Cretaceous, suggested by the similarity of sauropod remains found in these regions.

- When there were dinosaur migrations between Gondwana and Laurasia, the principal direction seems to have been northward.

SCATTERED REMAINS

- Discoveries of dinosaur remains in Alaska and in Antarctica in the 1980s showed that some dinosaurs lived in cold climates.

- Dinosaur fossils are limited to the remains of animals that lived on lowlands, close to rivers or streams. Upland animals are far from areas of deposition and so tend not to become fossilized.

- Sandy deserts are a great environment for dinosaur preservation. Many remains have been found of dinosaurs that were engulfed in sandstorms.

- The first Australian dinosaurs were found half way up a sea cliff in Victoria, in the 1980s. Their location posed a huge logistical problem for the paleontologists.

ONE CONTINENT
This model shows how the Earth would have looked sometime during the Triassic period. Dinosaurs would have roamed freely all over the single continent Pangaea. This helps to explain why the remains of the same, or very similar, dinosaurs are found in different parts of the world.

DINOSAUR FOSSILIZATION

- Actual dinosaur fossils are usually petrified bones, molds, or casts.

- Petrified dinosaur bones are produced when the original bone material has been replaced by minerals. The structure is exactly the same as the original.

- When the whole of the original animal has dissolved away, only a hole in the rock remains. This is called a mold.

- If the mold becomes filled with minerals, it produces a cast.

FLESH AND ORGANS

- Very rarely are parts of the soft anatomy of a dinosaur preserved.

- Some scientists argue that sauropods must have had several extra hearts in the neck, to allow them to pump blood all the way to the head. However, there is no hard evidence to support this.

- A skeleton of the ornithopod *Thescelosaurus*, found in South Dakota in 1993, has a structure that may be a heart.

- A baby theropod *Scipionyx* found in Cretaceous rocks in Italy shows traces of intestines, windpipe, and liver.

SCALY SKIN

This is the skin impression of a sauropod, probably a *Diplodocus*. The skin was made up of tightly packed scales with flexible edges, which allowed easy movement. This impression shows that the scales varied in size, the smaller ones occurring where the skin had to bend a lot.

COLORS AND SKIN

- It is impossible to determine the color of a dinosaur. Most colored restorations use colors based on modern animals such as lizards.

- Examples of preserved dinosaur skin are very rare, as it does not fossilize easily. The best examples are those of duckbills, which show a skin made up of a mosaic of nonoverlapping scales.

- *Pelecanimimus* is so-called because it was found preserved with a flap of skin under its throat – just like the pouch of a pelican.

- Impressions of skin found in the rock around fossils are much more common.

- The clearest skin impression from a big theropod is that of a South American *Carnotaurus* from the Cretaceous period.

MOUNTED SKELETONS

- A dinosaur reconstruction is a mounted skeleton of a dinosaur. They are displayed in museums to give people an idea of how dinosaurs looked.

- The first dinosaur reconstruction was made by sculptor Waterhouse Hawkins under the direction of Joseph Leidy. He assembled casts of the bones of *Hadrosaurus* in 1868, replacing the missing parts with plaster replicas.

Mounting a reconstruction of a dinosaur skeleton.

- Original fossil bones are extremely heavy. Modern reconstructions use lightweight casts to make the mounting easier, and the original bones are stored for research purposes.

- The American Museum of Natural History has the largest number of mounted dinosaur skeletons, with 21 on display.

DINOSAUR FACTS

LONG-NECKED PLESIOSAURS

- The long-necked group of plesiosaurs were the elasmosaurs. They swam with paddlelike legs, using an underwater flying motion like a penguin.

- Their eyes were big – good for finding prey in the dark waters. Their diet was mostly fish, but some of them may have sifted for food through mud on the seabed.

- The nostrils seem to have been too small for breathing. They were probably used for sensing their environment, and they breathed through their mouths.

- It is not known whether they gave birth to live young or laid eggs on beaches.

- *Hydrotherosaurus* was 39 ft (12 m) long. Half of that length was made up by its extended neck.

- Elasmosaurs evolved in the Triassic period and survived until the end of the Cretaceous.

SHORT-NECKED PLESIOSAURS

- The short-necked, big-headed plesiosaurs were the pliosaurs. They are regarded as the sperm whales of the Mesozoic era. They existed until the end of the Cretaceous period.

- Smaller types, like the 10-ft (3-m) long *Dolicorhynchops* probably fed on fish. The largest may have hunted elasmosaurs and ichthyosaurs.

- The biggest jawbone found is from *Liopleurodon*. It was 10 ft (3 m) long.

- Pliosaurs were probably ancestors of the elasmosaurs.

SEA MONSTER
Elasmosaurus (pictured left) displays the typical characteristics of the elasmosaurs – an extremely long neck, a small head, and four flippers. Large sea reptiles such as this dominated the oceans at the same time that the dinosaurs ruled the land.

ICHTHYOSAURS

- The ichthyosaurs were the most highly adapted of the Mesozoic sea reptiles. They had streamlined bodies, paddle limbs, a sharklike tail, and a dorsal fin.

- Triassic ichthyosaurs were huge and whalelike. Those from the Jurassic were smaller – about the size of dolphins.

- Belemnites – Mesozoic squidlike animals – formed much of their diet, as shown by fossilized tentacle hooks found in ichthyosaurs' stomach contents.

- They died away in the Cretaceous and were replaced by the mosasaurs.

MOSASAURS

- The mosasaurs were a group of swimming lizards from late Cretaceous times. They were close relatives of the modern monitor lizards.

- They mostly ate fish and shellfish. One type, *Globidens*, had broad teeth, well suited to crunching through hard shells.

- They moved their entire body and tail to swim and used their paddlelike limbs to stabilize themselves.

- Skin impressions suggest that the skin was scaly, like that of a snake.

- The biggest types of mosasaurs were about 33 ft (10 m) long.

SEA FOOD

Shellfish, such as the ammonite pictured here, were common in the seas of the Mesozoic Era. These are thought to have been the staple diet of some ancient sea reptiles. Ammonite shells have been found with tooth marks that match the bite of a mosasaur.

LONG-TAILED PTEROSAURS

- The pterosaurs were the flying reptiles of the age of dinosaurs. They were archosaurs, like the dinosaurs and crocodiles.

- They flew with leathery wings, supported by an elongated fourth finger. Strong fibers helped strengthen the wings.

- The earlier pterosaurs had long tails, narrow wings, and short wrists, and were called the rhamphorhynchoids. They evolved in the Triassic and survived until the end of the Jurassic.

- Most ate fish, but some of the smaller types would have eaten insects.

- The tails were stiff, straight rods reinforced by tendons. There was a paddle-shaped vane at the end.

SHORT-TAILED PTEROSAURS

- The later pterosaurs were the pterodactyloids. They succeeded the rhamphorhynchoids in the late Jurassic and survived until the end of the Cretaceous.

- The pterodactyloids had short tails, broad wings, and long wrists. There were many different types with various head shapes, mouths, and teeth.

- *Pterodactylus* had sharp teeth for catching fish; *Pterodaustro* had fine sieves for filtering plankton. *Pteranodon* had no teeth at all.

- The popular term "pterodactyl" is applied generally to both the pterodactyloids and the rhamphorhynchoids.

SKY REPTILES

The pterodactyloids – the short-tailed pterosaurs – were the largest animals that have ever flown in the Earth's skies. Some types, such as *Quetzalcoatlus* and *Arambourgiania*, had a wingspan of up to 39 ft (12 m) – as big as that of a small aircraft.

OTHER REPTILES AND AMPHIBIANS

- Big, crocodile-sized amphibians thrived until the mass extinction at the end of the Triassic. However, giant amphibian remains have been found in early Cretaceous rocks in Egypt.

- Modern amphibians – frogs and newts – date back to the Triassic, while lizards are known from Jurassic times.

- Snakes evolved in the Jurassic but were more common in the Cretaceous.

- Turtles evolved in the Triassic and flourished throughout the age of dinosaurs.

- Crocodiles have remained essentially unchanged since Triassic times.

- The big predators of the Triassic, rivaling the first dinosaurs, were the rauisuchians – giant land-dwelling crocodile-like animals.

Crocodiles are closely related to the dinosaurs.

MAMMALS

- The first mammals evolved at about the same time as the dinosaurs.

- Mammals were tiny and insignificant throughout the age of dinosaurs, a period that accounts for two-thirds of their evolutionary history.

- Early mammals were probably nocturnal insect eaters.

- They may have laid eggs, but suckled their young, as a modern duck-billed platypus does.

- Plant-eating mammals did not evolve until the late Jurassic. Some of these were about the size of modern-day beavers.

- Most of the primitive mammals became extinct at the end of the Cretaceous, along with the dinosaurs.

TRACE FOSSILS

FOOTPRINTS

- Fossil dinosaur footprints are far more common than fossil dinosaur bones.
- Dinosaur footprints are given their own scientific names because it is difficult to tell which particular animal made a particular footprint.
- Very few dinosaur tracks show marks of a tail, suggesting that dinosaurs walked with their tails off the ground.
- The speed of a dinosaur is estimated by comparing the length of the leg with the distance between footprints.

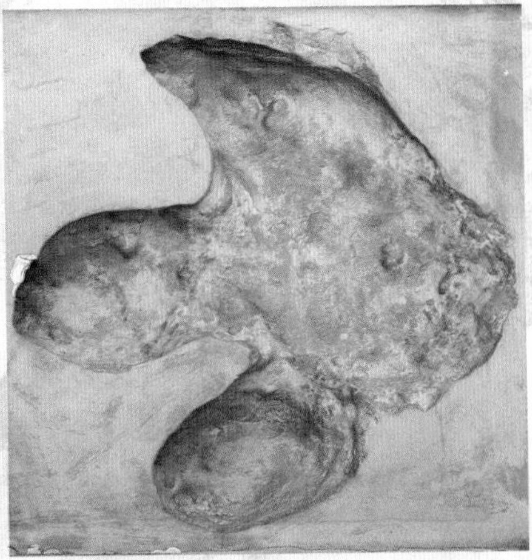

The fossilized footprint of an Iguanodon's left hind foot. This print was probably made by a youngster weighing about half a ton.

COPROLITES

- Coprolite is the name given to fossil dung. We can tell much about the diet of an extinct animal by studying coprolites.
- A coprolite attributed to *Tyrannosaurus* has fragments of duckbill bone incorporated in it.
- A large number of small coprolite pellets found in Yorkshire, England, each no bigger than a half inch in diameter, and containing cycad fragments, must have come from a dinosaur. Altogether they amounted to 7 cubic in (120 cubic cm) of dung – only dinosaurs were big enough to produce this amount.
- Spiral coprolites suggest that the animal had a spiral intestine.

DINOPATHOLOGY

- Some dinosaur remains show evidence of injury or disease. About a quarter of theropod remains show injury to the forelimbs, probably caused either while fighting or during mating.

- Broken and healed ribs in ceratopsians are seen in similar positions to those seen in male bison. This suggests that these animals butted each other's flanks.

- Many of the big dinosaurs have adjacent vertebrae fused together, possibly as a result of the stresses produced by the great weight of the animal.

- Ceratopsians are sometimes missing horns, perhaps as a result of fighting.

- The life expectancy of a dinosaur is hard to estimate. It has even been suggested that the big sauropods may have reached an age of around 200 years.

DINOSAUR EGGS

- As far as we know, all dinosaurs laid eggs. However, it has been suggested that dinosaurs with wide pelvises – sauropods and pachycephalosaurs – may have borne their young alive.

- Like footprints, dinosaur eggs are given their own scientific names, because it is so difficult to tell which dinosaur laid the egg.

- The name of a fossilized egg usually has "oo" in it. *Faveoloolithus* may be the egg of a sauropod. *Spheroolithus* may be the egg of a duckbill.

- Only if an embryo is preserved in the egg can it be firmly identified. So far, this has only been possible with *Troodon*, *Hypacrosaurus*, *Maiasaura*, and *Oviraptor*.

- A well-known fossil of *Compsognathus* was found to have fossil eggs around it. They are thought to have burst from its body during death.

A restoration of a Maiasaura nest.

FEEDING

- Plant-eating dinosaurs had jaws with very good leverage. The teeth were spaced closely together and sometimes overlapped. They had coarse, serrated edges and were mostly the same size.

- Meat-eating dinosaurs had widely spaced, tapered teeth. They were finely serrated (like steak knives) and were all of different sizes.

- Sauropods and prosauropods could not chew. They swallowed stones to grind up food in their gizzards.

- Ornithischians had grinding and chopping teeth, so they were able to chew their food held in their cheeks.

- *Allosaurus* had loosely articulated jaw bones, so that it could broaden its mouth and swallow huge chunks of meat.

This Tyrannosaurus *skeleton clearly shows the meat-eater's lethal teeth.*

SOUND, VISION, AND SMELL

- In the prosauropods, the sense of smell was quite acute, as shown by the nerve passages in the skull.

- It is thought that *Troodon* was able to perceive depth in vision – an advantage to a swift hunter.

- The tyrannosaurs had bones in their noses that increased the area of their sinuses. This indicates a powerful sense of smell.

- The acoustics of the skull of *Tyrannosaurus* suggest that it made a noise more like the croak of a frog than the roar of a lion.

- It is thought that forest-dwelling dinosaurs would have made high-pitched sounds that carried through the trees. Those that lived on the plains may have made deep sounds that would carry along the ground.

FAMILY LIFE

- We know that many dinosaurs lived in herds by the presence of bone beds and footprint tracks.

- The most famous nesting site is that of the duckbill *Maiasaura* found in Montana in the 1980s. All stages of growth were found, from eggs and hatchlings, to juveniles and adults.

- It is difficult to distinguish between male and female dinosaurs from their fossils. It is likely that females were larger than males and that males had more flamboyant frills and crests.

- A herd of sauropods may have moved in a formation that protected the young by keeping them in the middle.

- Ceratopsians may have formed a protective ring around their youngsters, with their horns pointing outward when danger threatened.

BRAINPOWER

The brainpower of a dinosaur is estimated by taking into account the weight of the body and the weight of the brain, and comparing it with that of the modern relative, the crocodile. This is called the encephalization quotient, or EQ. The larger the EQ the greater the brainpower. Typical EQs are as follows:

CREATURE	EQ
Sauropod	0.2
Ankylosaur	0.54
Stegosaur	0.58
Ceratopsian	0.7-0.9
Crocodile	1.0
Ornithopod	0.9-1.5
Big theropod	1.0-1.9
Small theropod	5.8

BIG-EYED HUNTER

Troodon had very large eyes and a relatively big brain. It is thought that its good vision and intelligence were the secrets of its success as a hunter. Scientists base this theory on the similarity of the optic nerve channels and brain cases of *Troodon* fossils with those of modern predatory creatures.

EXTINCTION THEORIES

There are many theories on why the dinosaurs died out. Here are some of the most commonly held ones:

- A meteorite or comet hit the Earth. The impact had a devastating effect, causing short-term phenomena such as tidal waves and wildfires, as well as long-term changes to the climate.

- Widespread volcanic activity, changing the atmosphere and climate.

- Gradual change in climate.

- Diseases spread by mixing populations.

- Cosmic rays from distant stars.

- Changes in vegetation resulting in starvation for herbivores.

- Environmental instability due to changing sea levels.

- Change in the Earth's magnetic field.

WARM BLOODED OR COLD BLOODED?

- The discovery of Deinonychus in the 1960s began the debate on whether dinosaurs were warm-blooded or cold-blooded. As a swift and agile predator, Deinonychus would probably have been warm-blooded.

- A warm-blooded animal needs about 10 times as much food as a cold-blooded animal.

- The small number of meat eaters compared to plant eaters in the Jurassic seems to suggest a warm-blooded mode of life.

- Some dinosaurs, such as Stegosaurus, had plates on their backs, possibly to collect heat from the Sun. This suggests cold-bloodedness.

- Some scientists think that the small theropods were warm-blooded and the big sauropods were cold-blooded.

Deinonychus - a warm-blooded dinosaur?

DINOSAURS AND FEATHERS

- Most scientists agree that dinosaurs are related to birds, but the exact relationship is not clear.

- The first known bird is Archaeopteryx from the late Jurassic. It was just like a little dinosaur covered in feathers.

  - The earliest birds have toothed jaws, long bony tails, and clawed fingers on the wings – all dinosaur features. Later birds had a mixture of these features and more traditional birdlike features.

  - In the early 1990s, some strange half-bird/half-dinosaur fossils were found in China. Sinosauripteryx was one of these – essentially a small theropod but covered in fine structures like feathers.

  - In 2001, a dromaeosaurid was found in China with what were undoubtedly feathers all over its body.

An artist's impression of Archaeopteryx.

"LIVING FOSSILS"

- No dinosaurs survive today, although there are occasional reports of Mesozoic-type animals being seen.

- The Loch Ness Monster and other mysterious lake creatures are reported to resemble plesiosaurs.

- The "Mokele-Mbembe" of the Congo region of Africa is purported to resemble a sauropod.

- The Leviathan and Behemoth mentioned in The Bible have been interpreted as early sightings of dinosaurs.

- The legend of the gryphon is thought to have originated in the discovery of the many fossil Protoceratops skulls that exist in Mongolia.

ANIMATING DINOSAURS

Several methods have been used to bring dinosaurs to life on the screen. They include:

- Using an actor in a costume, as in *The Land Unknown* (1957).

- Sticking horns and fins on living lizards to disguise them, as seen in *Journey to the Center of the Earth* (1958).

- Puppetry, in which a puppet is manipulated by off-screen operators, as in *The Land That Time Forgot* (1974).

- Computer-generated imagery, in which the visuals are created and animated by computer software. *Jurassic Park* (1993) is the best example of this.

DINOSAURS IN FILMS

- The first dinosaur in a film was in *Gertie the Dinosaur* (1912) in which a cartoon dinosaur on a film acted with a live actor on stage.

- The first full-length feature film to portray dinosaurs was *The Lost World* (1925).

- The most famous Japanese film dinosaur is *Godzilla*. The original Japanese spelling is *Gojira*, and was named after a technician in the studio.

- *Jurassic Park* (1993) was the first film to employ real paleontologists as advisers and to present dinosaurs as accurately as possible.

DINOSAURS IN ART AND LITERATURE

- The first novel to feature living fossil animals was Jules Verne's *Journey to the Center of the Earth* (1864).

- Possibly the best-known dinosaur novel was Arthur Conan Doyle's *The Lost World* (1912).

- The most famous dinosaur artist was Charles R. Knight (1874-1953). He worked with the best paleontologists of the time and his paintings are in many of the museums in the US.

- The first dinosaur textbook written for nonspecialists was *The Dinosaur Book*, written by paleontologist E.H.Colbert in 1945.

DINOSAUR FACTS

DINOSAUR THEME PARKS

- The first dinosaur amusement park was in Crystal Palace Park, London, where a number of statues of dinosaurs as well as a variety of other extinct animals were built in 1854.

- The first dinosaur amusement park in the United States was in Rapid City, South Dakota. It was constructed in the 1930s.

- The biggest dinosaur statue ever built to date is an incredible 150 feet (45 meters) long and 45 feet (13 meters) high. It is a sauropod and stands in San Gorgonio Pass in California. It is so big that a whole museum has been built inside it.

- The first-ever moving, life-sized dinosaur statues were built in 1933-1934 and appeared at the World's Fair in Chicago.

- An exhibition featuring the full-sized models from the film *Jurassic Park* toured the world after the release of the film.

DIGITAL DINOSAURS

The modern movie industry uses the very latest computer technology to bring dinosaurs to life. The creatures in this book featured in Disney's *Dinosaur*, released in 2000.

A scene from Jurassic Park

F A N T A S Y A N D F I C T I O N

DINOSAUR FACTS

THE FIRST...

- The first dinosaurs: *Eoraptor*, *Herrerasaurus*, and *Staurikosaurus*.

- The first ceratopsian: *Archaeoceratops*.

- The first ankylosaur: *Scelidosaurus*.

- The first dinosaur restoration: Gideon Mantell's drawing of Iguanodon in the 1820s.

- The first dinosaur film: *Gertie the Dinosaur*, made in 1912.

- The first discovery of a fossil sea reptile: *Mosasaurus* in 1766.

- The first description of a pterosaur: naturalist Cosimo Collini was the first to describe one of the flying reptiles in 1784.

THE BIGGEST AND LONGEST...

- The longest known dinosaur: *Seismosaurus*. It was up to 147 feet (45 m) in length.

- The biggest dinosaur overall: *Argentinosaurus* – at least 88 feet (27 m) long. It weighed 49.2 tons (50 tonnes).

- The longest dinosaur name: *Micropachycephalosaurus*.

- The biggest meat eater: either *Carcharodontosaurus* or *Giganotosaurus*; both of these massive theropods were up to 49 feet (15 m) long.

- The biggest head: *Torosaurus'*. This ceratopsian's head was around 9 feet (2.8 m) long, including its neck shield.

- The biggest eyes: *Dromiceiomimus'*. A relative of *Troodon*, it had eyes that were 3.9 in (10 cm) in diameter.

- The meat eater with the most teeth: *Baryonyx*. It had a total of 128 finely serrated teeth.

- The biggest bone: a sauropod hipbone measuring 6 ft by 4 ft (1.8 m by 1.4 m) and weighing 1500 lb (680 kg).

Giganotosaurus – *possibly the biggest meat-eating dinosaur.*

LONGEST NECK

The dinosaur with the longest neck was, not surprisingly, a sauropod. *Mamenchisaurus'* neck measured up to 32 feet (9.8 m) and contained 19 vertebrae. It made up almost half of the animal's total body length. Despite its enormous length, this dinosaur's neck was not particularly flexible.

THE SMALLEST...

- The smallest complete adult skeleton found: one of *Compsognathus*, measuring just 3.2 feet (1 m).

- The smallest complete infant skeleton: a *Mussaurus* skeleton, measuring 8 inches (20 cm).

- The smallest armoured dinosaur: *Scutellosaurus*, up to 4 feet (1.2 m) long.

- The shortest dinosaur name: *Minmi*.

- The smallest ceratopsian: *Microceratops* – only 23 inches (60 cm) long.

- The smallest footprint: that of an unnamed sparrow-sized dinosaur from Nova Scotia, Canada.

- The smallest brain: *Stegosaurus'* – it weighed about 2.5 oz (70 g).

Stegosaurus is well-known for having the smallest brain of any known dinosaur. It was about the size of a walnut.

DINOSAUR MISCELLANY

UNUSUAL NAMES

- *Atlascopcosaurus*, an Australian ornithopod, was named after the company that financed the expedition on which it was found.

- *Jurassosaurus nedegoapeferkimorum*, a Jurassic ankylosaur, has part of its name made up from the initials of the actors in the film *Jurassic Park*.

- *Masiakasaurus knopfleri*, a theropod from Madagascar, is named after the guitarist Mark Knopfler. The paleontologists were playing his music when they discovered it.

ALSO KNOWN AS...
Sometimes the same dinosaur is given a different name after separate discoveries of the same animal are made. In such cases, the rule is that the name given first is kept. The best known example of this was when *Brontosaurus* was renamed *Apatosaurus*.

Brontosaurus, *aka* Apatosaurus

- *Triceratops* was originally named *Bison alticornis*, because the remains were thought to have belonged to a buffalo.

PRONUNCIATION

There are no firm rules regarding the pronunciation of dinosaur names – different paleontologists pronounce the names in different ways. Here are some examples:

Diplodocus:	Di-**PLOD**-ocuss, or Diplo-**DOH** cuss
Troodon:	True-**OH**-don, or **TROO**don
Deinonychus:	Dino-**NYE**-cuss, or Di-**NONNY**-cuss
Ornithomimus:	Or-**NITH**-o-**MY**-muss, or Or-**NITH**-o-**ME**-muss
Euoplocephalus:	**YOU**-plo-**KEFF**-alus, or **YOU**-plo-**SEFF**-alus
Parasaurolophus:	Para-**SORROW**-lofus, or **PARA**-sor-**OLOF**-us
Iguanodon:	Ig-**WANNA**-don, or Ig-**YOU**-**ANNA**-don

"MISSING" DINOSAURS

Unfortunately, many important dinosaur finds have been lost. Here are just a few:

- Important specimens, including those of *Spinosaurus* and *Carcharodontosaurus*, found between 1910 and 1914 at El-Bahariya, Egypt, were destroyed when the museum in Munich in which they were housed was bombed during World War II.

- A sauropod vertebra that was reported in 1923 to have shown signs of cancer has now been lost. If true, it would be the only known occurrence of cancer in a dinosaur.

- The Allied bombing of Hamburg in World War II destroyed the best of the dinosaur statues in Hagenbeck's zoo.

- Two skeletons of *Corythosaurus* were lost when the ship they were on, the Mt. Temple, was sunk by a U-boat in 1916.

ANIMAL FEATURES

Some features of dinosaurs found in modern animals.

- The long neck of the typical sauropod is reflected in the long neck of the giraffe. In both cases, they allow the large animal to reach their food.

- The wide frill of a ceratopsian and the plates of a stegosaur may have had the same function as the tail of a peacock – that of attracting a mate.

- The legs of the fast dinosaurs such as *Troodon*, with short thighs to concentrate the muscle and long, lightweight shanks, are similar to those of fast-running mammals like deer.

Giraffes use their long necks to reach food in much the same way as the sauropods did.

- Lizards spread their rib cages flat over their basking rocks to soak up heat from the Sun. The spines on *Spinosaurus* and *Ouranosaurus* may have spread the skin for the same purpose.

REFERENCE SECTION

DINOSAUR DISCOVERERS

PEOPLE HAVE probably found dinosaur fossils for thousands of years. But it was not until 1841 that scientists first identified the dinosaur group. There have been many well-known dinosaur hunters, made famous because of the dinosaurs they have discovered.

SIR RICHARD OWEN (1804-1892) WAS a famous British anatomist. He coined the name "dinosaur," which means "terrible lizard."

WHAT HE DISCOVERED
Owen worked at the Natural History Museum in London, where he studied fossils found in Europe. He not only realized that some fossils were reptiles, but unknown types of giant reptiles. He concluded that they must have belonged to a group of extinct animals, and named this group dinosaurs.

DR. GIDEON MANTELL (1790-1852) was a medical doctor from Sussex in England. He was also a keen fossil hunter. He spent much of his early life collecting fossils in the hills near where he lived. But it was one fossil find that put his name in the history books.

WHAT HE DISCOVERED
In 1820, Gideon Mantell and his wife, Mary Ann, found some large teeth and bones in some gravel near a stone quarry. They belonged to an unknown, iguana-like animal. In 1825 he named it *Iguanodon*, although he did not realize at the time that it was a dinosaur.

DEAN WILLIAM BUCKLAND (1784-1856) was the first professor of geology at Oxford University in England. He was fascinated by fossils from childhood.

WHAT HE DISCOVERED
In 1824, a large jawbone with a giant tooth was found near Oxford. Buckland recognized it as belonging to a previously unknown giant reptile. This reptile was named *Megalosaurus*, which means "big lizard," and was the first dinosaur to be named. Like Mantell, Buckland did not know that *Megalosaurus* was a dinosaur.

JOHN BELL HATCHER (1861-1904) was a fossil collector for Othniel Marsh. Hatcher is recognized as one of the greatest collectors of dinosaurs in the history of American paleontology.

WHAT HE DISCOVERED
In 1888, Hatcher found part of a huge skull with horns beside the Judith River in Montana. It turned out to be a *Triceratops* skull, and was the first fossil of this dinosaur to be discovered. It was also the first of the horned dinosaurs to be found, which introduced a new dinosaur variety to paleontologists.

EDWARD DRINKER COPE (1840-1897) was an American from Philadelphia. He was a scientific genius, and dinosaurs were just one area on which he was an expert.

WHAT HE DISCOVERED
Cope started his scientific career after the American Civil War. He traveled with fellow scientist Othaniel Marsh on many of his early trips. They eventually became fierce rivals. Among his many finds, Cope discovered several primitive Triassic dinosaurs from New Mexico.

OTHNIEL CHARLES MARSH (1831-1899) was an American paleontologist born in New York. Along with E.D. Cope, Marsh was one of the great pioneers of dinosaur fossil hunting in the United States.

WHAT HE DISCOVERED
Marsh discovered many dinosaur fossil sites in the United States. The most famous were Como Bluff in Wyoming and several sites in Colorado. His intense rivalry with Edward Drinker Cope was nicknamed the "Bone Wars."

EBERHARD FRAAS (1862-1915) was a German paleontologist. He went on long expeditions to Africa in his search for dinosaurs fossils.

WHAT HE DISCOVERED
In 1907, Fraas was told of some dinosaur bones in a site in Tanzania, Africa. Fraas led an expedition set up to explore the site and, in 1909-12, the first fine specimens of *Kentrosaurus*, *Elaphrosaurus*, *Barosaurus*, and *Brachiosaurus* were discovered there. The *Brachiosaurus* skeleton Fraas discovered is now in a museum in Berlin, and is the largest mounted skeleton in the world.

GEORGE F. STERNBERG (1883-1969) WAS an American paleontologist who started collecting fossils at the age of six. He continued to work on fossils for the next 66 years.

WHAT HE DISCOVERED
George F. Sternberg made his most important dinosaur discovery in 1908: he was the first person to find an impression of dinosaur skin, which belonged to Anatosaurus. Sternberg made many other amazing discoveries, including the first fossil of *Edmontosaurus*.

EDWIN COLBERT (b.1905) is an American paleontologist and an expert in Triassic dinosaurs. He found the first dinosaur fossils in Antarctica. He has written several books about the history of dinosaurs.

WHAT HE DISCOVERED
Colbert found the first complete *Coelophysis* skeletons in New Mexico in 1947. Some skeletons held the bones of young *Coelophysis* in the rib cage. This indicated that *Coelophysis* may have been a cannibal.

ANDREW CARNEGIE (1835-1919) was originally from Scotland. He emigrated with his family to the United States at the age of 11. He made his fortune in the steel industry in Pittsburgh.

WHAT HE DISCOVERED
Carnegie set up the Carnegie Museum in Pittsburgh. He sent fossil hunters on long expeditions to find dinosaurs for his museum. They discovered two complete skeletons of *Diplodocus*. A replica of one of the skeletons stands in the Natural History Museum in London.

ROY CHAPMAN ANDREWS (1884-1960) led the first American expedition to the Gobi Desert in Mongolia in 1922. Andrews went with a team from the American Museum of Natural History (AMNH).

WHAT HE DISCOVERED
Andrews and his team discovered many new dinosaurs in the Gobi Desert. Among them were *Protoceratops*, *Velociraptor*, and *Oviraptor*. But the most significant find was some fossilized *Protoceratops* eggs – the first dinosaur eggs to be discovered.

EARL DOUGLASS (1862-1931) was an American from Utah. He worked at the Carnegie Museum in Pittsburgh.

WHAT HE DISCOVERED
In 1909 Douglass was sent by Andrew Carnegie to hunt for fossils in Utah. Douglass' discoveries included Diplodocus and *Apatosaurus*. The site where these dinosaurs were found was turned into the Dinosaur National Park, which still exists today.

BARNUM BROWN (1873-1963), an American, was hired by the American Museum of Natural History in New York because of his skill in finding dinosaur skeletons.

What he discovered
Barnum Brown's expertise in fossil hunting earned him the nickname "Mr. Bones." He found the first *Tyrannosaurus rex* fossils, and named *Ankylosaurus* and *Corythosaurus*. The AMNH houses the world's greatest display of Cretaceous dinosaurs as a result of Brown's collecting.

JIM JENSON (B.1910) is a self-taught paleontologist. He was the curator of the Vertebrate Paleontology Research Laboratory at Brigham Young University in Provo, Utah.

WHAT HE DISCOVERED
Jenson has discovered some of the largest dinosaurs. In 1972, he found a partial skeleton of a sauropod. He named it *Supersaurus*. Its height is estimated to be 54 ft (16.5 m). In 1979 he found a partial skeleton of another new sauropod. He named it Ultrasaurus, and it is thought to be even bigger than *Supersaurus*.

BILL WALKER (B. 1928) is a British quarry-worker who is also an amateur fossil collector. In 1982, he made an important dinosaur discovery when exploring a muddy clay pit in Surrey, England.

WHAT HE DISCOVERED
Walker found a huge claw, which broke into pieces when he held it. He took it to the British Museum in London, which organized an excavation to recover more of the creature. It turned out to be a new dinosaur, which was named *Baryonyx* walkeri, in honor of Walker.

REPTILES CLASSIFIED

ALL LIVING THINGS are classified into different groups, according to their common features. In the animal kingdom, vertebrates form a huge group. All vertebrates have a backbone – that is their common feature. This chart shows how reptiles, including the dinosaurs, fit into the vertebrate group.

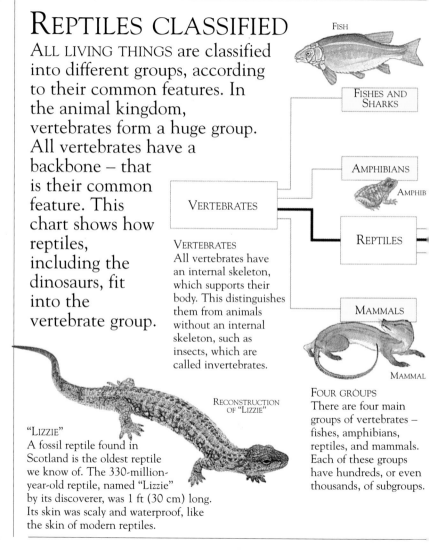

FISH

FISHES AND SHARKS

AMPHIBIANS

AMPHIB

VERTEBRATES

REPTILES

VERTEBRATES
All vertebrates have an internal skeleton, which supports their body. This distinguishes them from animals without an internal skeleton, such as insects, which are called invertebrates.

MAMMALS

MAMMAL

RECONSTRUCTION OF "LIZZIE"

"LIZZIE"
A fossil reptile found in Scotland is the oldest reptile we know of. The 330-million-year-old reptile, named "Lizzie" by its discoverer, was 1 ft (30 cm) long. Its skin was scaly and waterproof, like the skin of modern reptiles.

FOUR GROUPS
There are four main groups of vertebrates – fishes, amphibians, reptiles, and mammals. Each of these groups have hundreds, or even thousands, of subgroups.

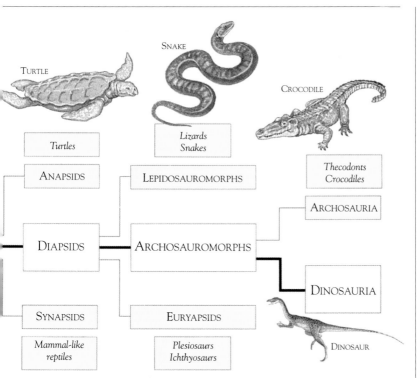

TURTLE

SNAKE

CROCODILE

Turtles

Lizards
Snakes

Thecodonts
Crocodiles

ANAPSIDS

LEPIDOSAUROMORPHS

ARCHOSAURIA

DIAPSIDS

ARCHOSAUROMORPHS

DINOSAURIA

SYNAPSIDS

EURYAPSIDS

Mammal-like
reptiles

Plesiosaurs
Ichthyosaurs

DINOSAUR

REPTILE GROUPS
The reptile group is divided into three subgroups. These three divisions are based on the number of openings in the skull behind the eye sockets.
The anapsids have no openings; the synapsids have one, and the diapsids have two.

DIAPSIDS
The diapsids are further divided into three groups. These are: lepidosauromorphs, which include lizards and snakes; archosauro-morphs, which include dinosaurs and crocodiles; and eurapsids, which include the plesiosaurs and the ichthyosaurs.

ARCHOSAUROMORPHS
The dinosaurs are in this group, as well as the thecodonts, which are thought to be the ancestors of the dinosaurs. Other members of the archosauromorph group include pterosaurs, crocodiles, and birds.

Dinosaurs classified

The classification of dinosaurs is controversial and is continually being revised. In this chart, dinosaurs are subdivided into three main groups – Herrerasauria (early predatory dinosaurs), Saurischia, and Ornithischia. Birds (Aves) are now considered to be dinosaurs because primitive birds, such as *Archaeopteryx*, shared many features in common with theropods.

ORNITHISCHIA

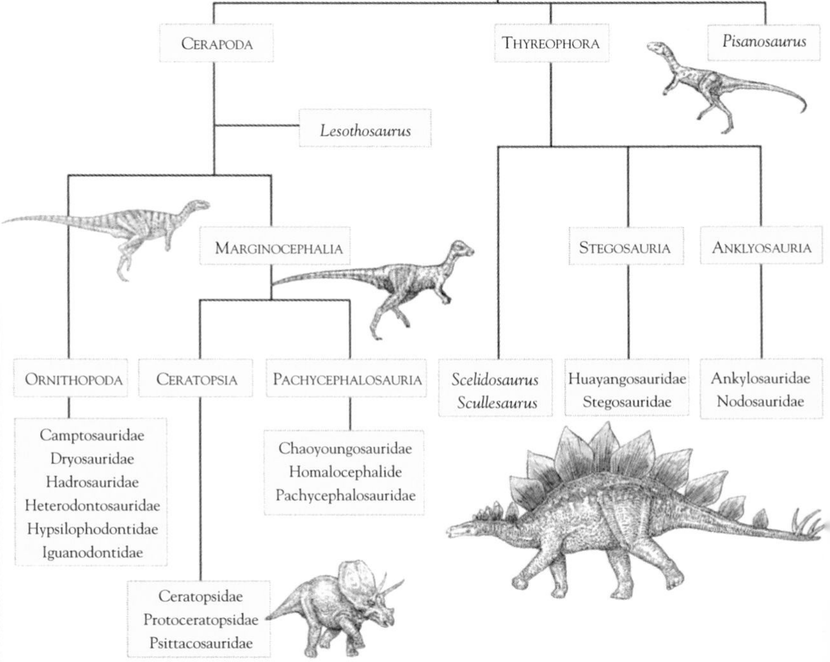

CERAPODA   THYREOPHORA   *Pisanosaurus*

Lesothosaurus

MARGINOCEPHALIA   STEGOSAURIA   ANKLYOSAURIA

| ORNITHOPODA | CERATOPSIA | PACHYCEPHALOSAURIA | *Scelidosaurus* *Scullesaurus* | Huayangosauridae Stegosauridae | Ankylosauridae Nodosauridae |

Camptosauridae
Dryosauridae
Hadrosauridae
Heterodontosauridae
Hypsilophodontidae
Iguanodontidae

Chaoyoungosauridae
Homalocephalide
Pachycephalosauridae

Ceratopsidae
Protoceratopsidae
Psittacosauridae

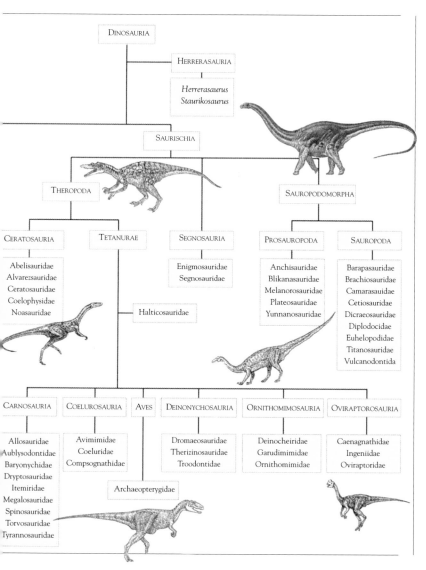

DINOSAURIA

HERRERASAURIA

Herrerasaurus
Staurikosaurus

SAURISCHIA

THEROPODA

SAUROPODOMORPHA

CERATOSAURIA

Abelisauridae
Alvarezsauridae
Ceratosauridae
Coelophysidae
Noasauridae

TETANURAE

Halticosauridae

SEGNOSAURIA

Enigmosauridae
Segnosauridae

PROSAUROPODA

Anchisauridae
Blikanasauridae
Melanorosauridae
Plateosauridae
Yunnanosauridae

SAUROPODA

Barapasauridae
Brachiosauridae
Camarasauidae
Cetiosauridae
Dicraeosauridae
Diplodocidae
Euhelopodidae
Titanosauridae
Vulcanodontida

CARNOSAURIA

Allosauridae
Aublysodontidae
Baryonychidae
Dryptosauridae
Itemiridae
Megalosauridae
Spinosauridae
Torvosauridae
Tyrannosauridae

COELUROSAURIA

Avimimidae
Coeluridae
Compsognathidae

AVES

Archaeopterygidae

DEINONYCHOSAURIA

Dromaeosauridae
Therizinosauridae
Troodontidae

ORNITHOMIMOSAURIA

Deinocheiridae
Garudimimidae
Ornithomimidae

OVIRAPTOROSAURIA

Caenagnathidae
Ingeniidae
Oviraptoridae

RECORDS AND MYTHS

As SCIENCE HAS ADVANCED, so has our understanding of dinosaurs. With almost every new discovery, we learn more about these giant reptiles. The early dinosaur experts had beliefs about dinosaurs which we now know to be incorrect. The largest, smallest, fastest, most intelligent, or the least intelligent dinosaur also changes as our knowledge increases.

DINOSAUR RECORDS

• The smallest dinosaur ever found was called *Mussaurus*. It was only 8 in (20 cm) long, but the single skeleton found may have been a hatchling. The smallest adult dinosaur we know of was *Compsognathus*, which was about the size of a chicken.

• *Dromiceiomimus* may have been the fastest of the dinosaurs, running at speeds of over 43 mph (70 km/h).

• The sauropod Mamenchisaurus had the longest neck of any dinosaur. The length of the neck was around 46 ft (14 m).
• *Tyrannosaurus rex* was the largest meat-eating dinosaur that ever lived. It was about 46 ft (14 m) long, and 18 ft (6 m) high. Its powerful jaws had teeth as long as 7 in (18 cm).
• The biggest dinosaur that we know of was the sauropod Seismosaurus. It was about 131 ft (40 m) long and weighed about 51 tons (tonnes).

• The herbivorous hadrosaurs had about 960 teeth – more than any other dinosaurs. That was about 480 tightly packed teeth in each jaw.

• *Troodon* had the largest brain in proportion to its size of any dinosaur.
• *Stegosaurus* had the smallest brain in proportion to its size.
• *Diplodocus* had the longest tail of all the dinosaurs, at over 43 ft (13 m) in length.

DINOSAUR MYTHS

• In 1822, Gideon Mantell made a reconstruction of *Iguanodon*, based on the few bones he had found. He had only one thumb spike, which he thought belonged on *Iguanodon's* nose. This was similar to the nose spike of an iguana, after which *Iguanodon* was named. It was not until the discovery of several skeletons in the late 1800s that scientists realized this mistake.

• In China, the word "konglong" means both "dinosaur" and "terrible dragon." The Chinese have been collecting dinosaur fossils for 2,000 years. Since the third century A.D., and perhaps before then, the Chinese believed that dinosaur bones were actually the remains of dragons.

• Many films and books portray dinosaurs and humans as living at the same time. In fact, dinosaurs became extinct over 60 million years before the first humans appeared.

• It used to be thought that all dinosaurs dragged their tails on the ground, like modern lizards. Some sauropods probably did, but most dinosaurs had stiffened tails, which they held horizontally off the ground.

• *Hypsilophodon* was once thought to have lived in trees. It was believed that their long tails helped them to balance in the branches, and their sharp claws were used for clinging. We now know their fingers and toes were not designed for gripping branches.

• Many people think that dinosaurs were all huge and cumbersome. But the vast majority were only about as big as an elephant, and some were as small as a chicken. Most were very agile, too.

• It was thought that Brachiosaurus lived in water because of the high position of its nostrils. But the great water pressures at depth would not have allowed it to breathe.

• *Iguanodon* was the first dinosaur to be reconstructed. At first it was shown as a slow, sprawling lizard, dragging a fat belly on the ground. We now know that *Iguanodon* was actually bipedal and much slimmer.

DIGGING UP DINOSAURS

MANY IMPORTANT dinosaur discoveries are made by professional and amateur collectors. Once discovered, fossil bones should be removed only by experienced professionals, because the bones are often fragile. The method of removing the bones depends on a number of factors, but generally follows a similar procedure.

1 SITE
Once a dinosaur site has been uncovered, the fossil bones have to be excavated (dug up). This delicate operation is carried out using special tools.

2 EXCAVATION
Hammers, chisels, and picks are used to remove most of the matrix (earth and stone material surrounding the bones).

3 EXPOSING THE BONES
Whenever possible, the matrix is removed close to the bone. This is done with great care so as to not damage the bone. The bones are exposed to reveal their full size so that no fragment will be left behind when removed.

5 JACKET ON OTHER SIDE
Once the exposed part of the bone has been coated, the rest of the bone, including some of the matrix, can be dug out of the ground. It is then covered with a plaster and burlap jacket.

4 PLASTER JACKET
The exposed part of the bones are coated with glue and covered with a jacket of plaster and burlap (a type of canvas). This will protect the bones as they travel from the site to a museum, where they can be studied in more detail.

6 REMOVAL FROM SITE
The jacketed bones are sometimes so big and heavy that a crane is needed to lift them onto a truck.

Resources

ARGENTINA

Museum of La Plata University
La Plata

AUSTRALIA

Queensland Museum
Gregory Terrace
Fortitude Valley
Queensland 4006

Museum of Victoria
328 Swanston Street
Melbourne
Victoria 3000

Australian Museum
College Street
Sydney
New South Wales 2000

AUSTRIA

Natural History Museum
1 Marcia-Theresien-Platz
Vienna

BELGIUM

Royal Institute of Natural Sciences
Rue Vautier 29
B-1040 Brussels

CANADA

Canadian Museum of Nature
National Museum of Canada
240 McLeod Avenue
Ottawa
Ontario K1A 0MB

Royal Ontario Museum
100 Queen's Park
Toronto
Ontario M5S 2C

INDIA

Geology Museum
Indian Statistical Institute
Calcutta

ITALY

Municipal Museum of Natural History
S. Croce 1730
30125 Venice

JAPAN

National Science Museum
Tokyo

MEXICO

Natural History Museum
Mexico City

NEW ZEALAND

Canterbury Museum
Rolleston Avenue
Christchurch 1

POLAND

Dinosaur Park
Chorzow, Silesia
Institute of Palaeobiology
Al Zwirki I Wigury 93
02-089 Warsaw

RUSSIA

Palaeontological Institute
Academy of Science
Moscow 117321

Central Geological and Prospecting Museum
St Petersburg

SOUTH AFRICA

South African Museum
Cape Town

Bernard Price Institute
for Palaeontological
Research
University of
Witwaterstrand
Jan Smuts Avenue
Johannesburg 2001

SPAIN

**Natural Science
Museum**
Madrid

SWEDEN

**Palaeontological
Museum**
Uppsala University
751 05 Uppsala

UNITED KINGDOM

Ulster Museum
Botanic Gardens
Belfast BT9 5AB

Birmingham Museum
Chamberlain Square
Birmingham B3 3DH

Museum of Geology
Cambridge University
Downing Street
Cambridge CB2 3EQ

**National Museum of
Wales**
Cathays Park
Cardiff CF1 3NP

The Dinosaur Museum
Icen Way
Dorchester
Dorset DT1 1EW

**National Museums of
Scotland**
Chambers Street
Edinburgh EH1 1JF

Hunterian Museum
University of Glasgow
University Avenue
Glasgow G12 8QQ

Leicestershire Museums
96 New Walk
Leicester LE1 6TD

**British Museum
(Natural History)**
Cromwell Road
London SW7 5BD

Crystal Palace Park
Sydenham
London SE20

Maidstone Museum
Faiths Street
Maidstone
Kent ME14 1LH

University Museum
Parks Road
Oxford OX1 3PW

**Museum of Isle of
Wight**
Sandown Library
High Street
Sandown
Isle of Wight PO35 8AF

UNITED STATES

**American Museum of
Natural History**
Central Park West/
79th Street
New York NY 10024

**Carnegie Museum of
Natural History**
4400 Forbes Avenue
Pittsburgh
Pennsylvania 15213

**Field Museum of
Natural History**
Roosevelt Road at Lake
Shore Drive
Chicago
Illinois 60605

**Peabody Museum of
Natural History**
Yale University
170 Whitney Avenue
New Haven
Connecticut 06511

Pronunciation guide

REFERNCE

ALBERTOSAURUS
(al-BERT-oh-SORE-us)

ALLOSAURUS
(al-oh-SORE-us)

ANCHISAURUS
(AN-ki-SORE-us)

ANKYLOSAURUS
(an-KIE-loh-SORE-us)

APATOSAURUS
(ah-PAT-oh-SORE-us)

ARCHAEOPTERYX
(ark-ee-OP-ter-iks)

BAROSAURUS
(bar-oh-SORE-us)

BARYONYX
(bar-ee-ON-iks)

BRACHIOSAURUS
(brak-ee-oh-SORE-us)

CARNOTAURUS
(kar-noh-TOR-us)

CENTROSAURUS
(SEN-troh-SORE-us)

CERATOSAURUS
(seh-rat-oh-SORE-us)

CETIOSAURUS
(see-tee-oh-SORE-us)

CHASMOSAURUS
(kaz-moh-SORE-us)

COELOPHYSIS
(SEEL-oh-FIE-sis)

COMPSOGNATHUS
(komp-soh-NAY-thus)

CORYTHOSAURUS
(koh-rith-oh-SORE-us)

CRIORHYNCHUS
(cry-oh-RINK-us)

CRYPTOCLIDUS
(cript-oh-CLIE-dus)

DASPLETOSAURUS
(das-PLEE-toh-SORE-us)

DEINOCHEIRUS
(DINE-oh-KEE-rus)

DEINONYCHUS
(die-NON-i-kus)

DIMORPHODON
(die-MORF-oh-don)

DIPLODOCUS
(di-PLOH-de-kus)

DROMAEOSAURUS
(DROH-may-oh-SORE-us)

DROMICEIOMIMUS
(droh-MEE-see-oh-MEEM-us)

EDMONTONIA
(ed-mon-TONE-ee-ah)

EDMONTOSAURUS
(ed-MON-toh-SORE-us)

EORAPTOR
(EE-oh-RAP-tor)

EUOPLOCEPHALUS
(you-op-loh-SEF-ah-lus)

EUSTREPTOSPONDYLUS
(yoo-STREP-toh-SPON-die-lus)

GALLIMIMUS
(gal-lee-MEEM-us)

GRYPOSAURUS
(GRIPE-oh-SORE-us)

HADROSAURUS
(HAD-roh-SORE-us)

HERRERASAURUS
(eh-ray-rah-SORE-us)

HETERODONTOSAURUS
(HET-er-oh-DONT-oh-SORE-us)

HYPACROSAURUS
(high-PAK-roh-SORE-us)

HYPSILOPHODON
(hip-sih-LOH-foh-don)

ICTHYOSAURUS
(IKH-thee-oh-SORE-us)

IGUANODON
(ig-WHA-noh-don)

INGENIA
(in-GAY-nee-a)

KENTROSAURUS
(KEN-troh-SORE-us)

LAMBEOSAURUS
(LAMB-ee-oh-SORE-us)

184

MAIASAURA
(MY-ah-SORE-ah)

MAMENCHISAURUS
(mah-MEN-chee-SORE-us)

MASOSAURUS
(MAZ-oh-SORE-us)

MASSOSPONDYLUS
(MAS-oh-SPON-die-lus)

MEGALOSAURUS
(MEG-ah-loh-SORE-us)

MELANOROSAURUS
(MEL-an-or-oh-SORE-us)

MURAENOSAURUS
(mure-rain-oh-SORE-us)

MUSSAURUS
(mus-OR-us)

MUTTABURRASAURUS
(MUT-a-BUR-a-SORE-us)

ORNITHOLESTES
(OR-nith-OH-LES-teez)

ORNITHOMIMUS
(OR-ni-thoh-MEE-mus)

OURANOSAURUS
(OO-ran-oh-SORE-us)

OVIRAPTOR
(OHV-ih-RAP-tor)

PACYCEPHALOSAURUS
(PAK-ee-SEF-a-loh-
SORE-US)

PARASAUROLOPHUS
(par-a-SORE-oh-LOAF-us)

PELONEUSTES
(pel-oh-nee-OOST-ees)

PINACOSAURUS
(pin-AK-oh-SORE-us)

PLATEOSAURUS
(PLAT-ee-oh-SORE-us)

PLIOSAURUS
(plie-oh-SORE-us)

POLACANTHUS
(pol-a-KAN-thus)

PRENOCEPHALE
(pren-oh-SEF-a-lee)

PSITTACOSAURUS
(Si-tak-oh-SORE-us)

PTERANODON
(teh-RANN-oh-don)

PTERODACTYLUS
(teh-roh-DACT-illus)

QUETZALCOATLUS
(kwet-zal-COAT-lus)

RHAMPHORHYNCHUS
(RAM-foh-RING-khus)

RIOJASAURUS
(ree-O-ha-SORE-us)

SALTASAURUS
(sal-te-SORE-us)

SAUROPELTA
(SORE-oh-PEL-ta)

SEISMOSAURUS
(SIZE-moh-SORE-us)

SHONISAURUS
(shon-ee-SORE-us)

SORDES
(SOHR-deez)

STEGOCERAS
(ste-GOS-er-as)

STEGOSAURUS
(STEG-oh-SORE-us)

STENOPTERYGIUS
(sten-OP-teh-RIDGE-ee-us)

STRUTHIOMIMUS
(STRUTH-ee-oh-
MEEM-us)

STYGIMOLOCH
(STIJ-i-MOH-lok)

STYRACOSAURUS
(sty-RAK-oh-SORE-us)

SUPERSAURUS
(SUE-per-SORE-us)

TOROSAURUS
(tor-oh-SORE-us)

TRICERATOPS
(try-SERRA-tops)

TROODON
(TROH-oh-don)

TUOJIANGOSAURUS
(toh-HWANG-oh-
SORE-us)

TYRANNOSAURUS
(tie-RAN-oh-SORE-us)

ULTRASAURUS
(ul-tra-SORE-us)

VELOCIRAPTOR
(vel-O-si-RAP-tor)

Glossary

AMPHIBIANS
A group of animals that are able to live both on land and in water.

ANKYLOSAURS
Quadrupedal, armored ornithischians.

ARMORED DINOSAURS
Dinosaurs whose bodies were protected by bony plates or spikes. These included ankylosaurs and some sauropods.

ARCHOSAUROMORPHS
A major group of reptiles which includes dinosaurs, thecodonts, pterosaurs, crocodiles, and birds.

BIPEDAL
Walking on the two hind legs only.

CARNIVORE
An animal that eats meat.

CARNOSAURS
A group of large theropods.

CERATOPSIANS
Quadrupedal ornithischians. Most ceratopsians had heads decorated with horns and frills.

CLASSIFICATION
The process of arranging animals into groups, related by common physical features.

COLD-BLOODED
Dependent on conditions outside the body for temperature regulation, such as the Sun's heat, to give warmth to the body.

CONIFERS
Trees that bear cones, such as pines and firs.

CONTINENTAL DRIFT
The constant movement of the plates which make up the Earth's lithosphere.

CRETACEOUS PERIOD
The third period of the Mezozoic era – 65-145 million years ago.

DIAPSID
A reptile group which includes the archosauromorphs, the lepidosauromorphs, and the euryapsids.

DINOSAURS
An extinct group of archosauromorphs with an erect stance. They

included the ancestors of modern birds.

EURYAPSIDS
A reptile group which includes the two groups of sea reptiles: plesiosaurs and ichthyosaurs.

EXTINCTION
The process by which living things die out of existence.

FOSSIL
The preserved remains of something that once lived.

GASTROLITHS
Stones that are swallowed to help grind up food in the stomach.

HADROSAURS
Large ornithopods with ducklike bills, of which there were two groups: lambeosaurines and hadrosaurines.

HERBIVORE
An animal that feeds on plants.

INVERTEBRATES
Animals without a backbone.

ISCHIUM
One of the two lower hipbones of dinosaurs

(the other was the pubis). The ischium anchored muscles that worked the hind legs.

JURASSIC PERIOD
The second period of the Mesozoic era – 145-208 million years ago.

LITHOSPHERE
The Earth's crust and upper mantle. It is approximately 124 miles (200 km) thick.

MESOZOIC ERA
The period of time between 65-245 million years ago. The Mesozoic era incorporated the Triassic, Jurassic, and Cretaceous periods.

ORNITHISCHIANS
The "bird-hipped" dinosaurs. One of the two major groups of dinosaurs.

ORNITHOPODS
Small to very large plant-eating ornithischians that were mostly bipedal.

PACHYCEPHALOSAURS
Bipedal ornithopods. Also known as bone-headed dinosaurs, because the roof of their skull was very thick.

PALEONTOLOGIST
A person who studies fossils.

PROSAUROPODS
Small to large early sauropodomorphs.

PTEROSAURS
The flying reptiles of the Mesozoic era. Distant cousins of the dinosaurs.

PUBIS
One of the two lower hipbones of dinosaurs (the other was the ischium). In some dinosaurs, the pubis anchored the muscle that pulled the hind legs forward.

QUADRUPEDAL
Walking on all four legs.

REPTILES
A group of "cold-blooded" vertebrates with scaly skin.

SAURISCHIANS
The "lizard-hipped" dinosaurs. One of the two major groups of dinosaurs.

SAUROPODOMORPHS
A group of quadrupedal herbivorous dinosaurs with long tails and necks. This group included the largest land animals that ever lived.

SAUROPODS
Large to immense sauropodomorphs.

STEGOSAURS
Quadrupedal ornithischians with two rows of plates and/or spines running along the neck, back, and tail.

SYNAPSIDS
A reptile group that includes mammallike reptiles (they are distantly related to mammals).

THECODONTS
A group of archosauromorphs which are the ancestors of the dinosaurs.

THEROPODS
Bipedal, carnivorous saurischian dinosaurs.

TRIASSIC PERIOD
The first period of the Mesozoic era – 208-245 million years ago.

VERTEBRAE
Bones of the spinal column.

VERTEBRATES
Animals with backbones.

WARM-BLOODED
Maintaining body warmth by turning the energy gained by food into heat.

Index

Acknowledgements

Dorling Kindersley would like to thank:
Hilary Bird for the index. Esther Labi and Robert Graham for editorial assistance. Carnegie Museum of Natural History for use of *Apatosaurus* skeleton on pages 88/89.

Photographs by:
Paul Bricknell, Andy Crawford, John Douns, Lynton Gardiner, Steve Gorton, Colin Keates, Gary Kevin, Dave King, William Lindsay, Ray Moller, Miguel Periera, Tim Ridley, Dave Rudlan, Bruce Selyen, Paul Sereno, Harry Taylor, Jerry Young

Illustrations by:
Roby Braun, Lynn Chadwick, Simone End, Eugene Fleury, Giuliano Fornari, Steve Kirk, Janos Marffy, Ikkyu Murakawa, Andrew Robinson, Graham Rosewarne, John Sibbick, John Temperton, John Woodcock.

Picture credits: t = top b = bottom c = centre l= left r = right
American Natural History Museum 172tl; 173 cl, Roby Braun 64tr. Fortean 124tl.
Frank Lane Picture Library/Eric and David Hosking 53tr.
Hulton Picture Library 16tl; 170tl. Image Bank/Robert Hardrie 133tl. Kobal 21tl. Ikkyu Murakawa 112cl; 112cr.
Museum of the Rockies/Bruce Selyem 55tr; 74 75c; 182tl; 182bl; 182r; 183l; 183tr; 183br.
Natural History Museum, London 21br; 100cr; 103tl; 168.
Science Photo Library/Julian Baum 132 bl. John Sereno 56tr. John Sibbick 53br; 104bl.

Every effort has been made to trace the copyright holders and we apologise in advance for any unintentional omissions. We would be pleased to insert the appropriate acknowledgement in any subsequent edition of this publication.